# OUT OF HIDING

# OUT OF HIDING

KASSIANA "TANA" BATEMAN

Charleston, SC
www.PalmettoPublishing.com

*Out of Hiding*

First Edition

Paperback ISBN: 979-8-88590-366-0
eBook ISBN: 979-8-88590-367-7

# In memory of

*Family Herrmann and Mr. Schragenheim*

# Dedication

I HAVE TO THANK SOME PEOPLE who made it possible for me to write this book. My friends Heiner and Ilse Herrmann were the first people who suggested that I should write this book. Unfortunately they are not with us anymore, and neither is my mentor Hans Schragenheim. But my son, Lee, his wife, Diana, and my granddaughter, Maya, support me in every way. I met some people along the way that encouraged me and made suggestions for this book. Thank you to Joceline Lemair, Jack my very special friend (you know who you are), whose opinion means a lot to me, and his daughter, Denise Sharp, who suggested my publisher. My friend Father "SOB" (it's a joke between a priest and me) helped with the wording. Without Tammy Marlin and Rose Porcelli, I never would have been able to do all the computer work, and they were there for me whenever I asked for help. And of course, my son Lee who edited the whole book. I would also like to mention the country Israel: without this country, and without living there, I would have never found and befriended the people that were so helpful to me in making good choices, including my husband, Jessie Jackson Bateman, whom I met in Israel and who brought me to the United States of America.

# Foreword

FORTUNATELY, THANKS TO MY very good friends in Israel, I have been able to change my stars, and from my beginning as a rough, hard, defensive person that felt that the world was against me, and as a survivor of the Holocaust, I have been able to find the good in myself. As a result I was able to stop hiding and have shared this goodness through more than twenty years of rewarding volunteer work as a counselor for a crisis line. I have been able to give to others from my life experience. I have worked with the homeless and youth suicide prevention, become a speaker for the United Way Speakers Bureau, and received numerous awards. People were grateful to have someone listen to their problems, understand them, and if at all possible assist and help. What can be more rewarding than to be able to help those who need that help?

Stephen Spielberg is one more reason why I want to write my story.

Making *Schindler's List* was a life-changing experience for Stephen Spielberg. Encountering the real people and the real stories portrayed in the film caused him to realize how much of a Jew he really is. His mother was very happy about his awakening.

After making *Schindler's List*, Stephen Spielberg wanted to let the world know the stories of the children who were born during the Holocaust and who survived the Holocaust. As I am one of these children, Spielberg's team of interviewers came to my house and videotaped the telling of my story. This tape is now in the Stephen Spielberg Museum of the Shoah, the Hebrew word for Holocaust, in Los Angeles. Mr. Spielberg also sent me a copy of the tape along with a personal letter thanking me for my time and for telling my story. If he found it interesting enough to tape my story, then I think that it is interesting enough to write my story about what it took to come *Out of Hiding*.

So many people in my life helped me to come out of the dark and out of hiding, which took years. Without my friends the Herrmann family, which included Miriam and Nurit the daughters, in Israel, and without my mentor Hans Schragenheim, I would never have achieved anything, because in Germany I would have remained a "nothing." I think one has to go through the dark to see the light and find a way to reach that light, which could be very far away, but no matter how difficult and long the road is and how far away the light seems to be, one must keep on striving.

I grew up poor and way undereducated without any family support. I did not have a family since we are Jews—they were taken away and murdered by the Nazis of the Third Reich in concentration camps. Since I never knew what family life was like, I had nobody to look up to and lean on or trust. I have been through the darkest places of my life alone and without love, without somebody who believed in me, to listen to or talk to. Therefore I made many mistakes, which sometimes were very costly and almost cost my life several times. I knew there was something out there and I just had to find it, which I did.

Today I speak five languages, of which I read and write three, and have traveled to more than fifty countries.

My son, Lee, sent me an email while I was on my last trip to Israel:

"My mom has crossed the Atlantic and Mediterranean and landed in Tel Aviv, Israel, which was the first real place she could call home. She moved there at twenty-one from war-torn post-Holocaust Germany, not knowing anyone, not knowing Hebrew. She was drawn to it.

"She made lifelong friends there. She met my dad while he was consulting with the Israeli Air Force on behalf of the US government. Without Israel I guess I wouldn't be here. Her spirit needs it. Twenty-five hours of travel is tough at her age, but it'll be worth it all as soon as she hugs her best friend, Nurit Segura.

"I hope you have a beautiful experience returning home. I love you very much."

My son, Lee, and my granddaughter, Maya, support me in writing my story. So does my friend and part-time advisor, Joceline Lemair, who spent so many hours helping me with this book and giving me directions.

Thank you to all those who have been and those who are still in my life.

I love you all.

# My Family's Life in Germany before World War II

Long before Hitler was born into this world, my Jewish family had very happy and funny times and memories worth telling. Of course, after Hitler took over, there was very little happiness left for any Jewish family. So let's start with the memories and stories my mother told me about our family. I heard them so many times. It almost feels as if I were there when the stories my mother told me actually happened.

The only members of the Friedlaender family and the Hirsch family from my mother's side that survived the Nazi time were my mother, me, a born Hirsch, and Uncle Emil, my grandmother's brother, who was a Friedlaender, and his wife. (Emil married a woman who supposedly was of ill repute and a Catholic, but who helped Emil, the husband, to survive the Nazi time.) Emil and his wife had no children. (He was the sleaziest, most disgusting person I ever met in my life. This will become clearer later on, in the history of these pages).

My great-grandfather was the owner of a bakery, which provided the breakfast rolls for the Kaiser Hof (royal household). He was permitted to have a shingle hanging outside his bakery saying "KAISERLICHE HOF BAECKEREI" (bakery of the royal household). They delivered the freshly baked breakfast rolls every morning to the Charlottenburg Schloss, which is located in a relatively busy area in Berlin. At one time I lived right behind that *Schloss* (castle), which had a huge park as part of the royal grounds. Of course when I walked through the royal garden in my teens, there was no kaiser occupying the castle.

–

MY GREAT-GRANDFATHER'S BUSINESS was booming—it was a very prestigious bakery that specialized in breads and beautiful cakes.

His daughters were responsible for delivering those freshly baked rolls to the castle's kitchen every morning.

One day, Else, the younger daughter, delivered the rolls, and as she was walking through the royal garden, a young man walked up to her, inquiring what she was doing. When she explained that she delivered the breakfast rolls, he took her in his arms and kissed her, and she was very perplexed and slapped him, not knowing who he was. That same afternoon Else received a bouquet of roses and a large box of chocolates. When she read the card that came with this delivery it read as follows:

"Thank you for the kiss—HRH Prince Wilhelm" (His Royal Highness Prince Wilhelm, the future kaiser of Germany). This became one of the favorite stories to tell over and over—as you can see, it is still alive today, passed on through the generations. (I told this story to *my* granddaughter Maya).

Another lovely story is how my great-grandmother met her husband.

This young man came to shop at the bakery every day, but nobody paid attention to him, since the bakery was a very well-established business and very busy. One day he asked to speak to the owner of the shop, to my great-grandfather, whose last name was Friedlaender. He indeed came to see this customer and asked how he could help him. The man introduced himself as Siegfried Friedlaender, yes, the same last name and no relation, not just yet. And here is what happened.

Siegfried Friedlaender introduced himself and pointed to one of the pictures that were placed on a shelf behind the counter, and he asked, "May I know who this young lady is?" And it was explained to him that this was Selma, my great-grandfather's oldest daughter (he had five).

"Why?" asked my great-grandfather.

Siegfried pulled out official papers that showed who he was and what his wealth was to prove that he could easily take care of a family. He said, "I am in love with her, and I want to marry her."

My great-grandfather called for his daughter and introduced her to Siegfried Friedlaender and said, "This man wants to marry you. Do you want to marry him?"

And even though they had never met before, very shyly, Selma said, "Yes."

They married and had six children: two girls and four boys. Selma called her husband Siegelchen all through their marriage. She was almost 6' tall, and Siegelchen was only about 5'7". Siegelchen always said he married the most expensive women to be his wife, because everything she wore had to be especially made for her, including shoes; what store carried a size 13 female shoe? Even her undergarments were made for her.

People would whisper behind their backs, and they were aware of that, but Siegelchen and Selma had a very happy and long marriage with their six children. The boys were named Albert, Emil, Richard, and Max, and the two girls were named Else and Jenni. There was a seventh child, but he died at childbirth. Jenni was my grandmother and the older one of the girls.

After Selma was widowed, she moved in with my grandmother until she passed away. My mother knew her grandmother only from her early childhood.

Everything I know about my great-grandparents and grandparents was because my mother told me so much about them and repeated these stories numerous times. My mother loved her family and loved to retell the stories about them. For her, it was reliving her past and a happy childhood with the family she loved so much. She was so fortunate to have grown up in this wonderful family. That was something I always wanted for myself growing up but never had, thanks to the Nazis, who killed almost all my family, that I never had met. Unfortunately, there are no diaries or letters to prove any of these stories to be correct, but my mother never deviated from telling any of these stories. My mother never met her grandfather, or at least not that she could remember.

The other story my mother used to tell me was that her grandparents had coffee and cake every afternoon at 3:00 p.m. on the dot, on the balcony, weather permitting. My mother's grandfather, Siegfried (Siegelchen) Friedlaender would say every time, and I mean every time, when they had coffee on the balcony, "Selma, we should paint a palm scenery on the wall of the balcony," and Selma answered every time, and I mean every time, "No, Siegelchen, we are not painting palm scenery on the balcony wall."

This went on for years, according to my mother, who heard this story from her mother. So one day Siegelchen again said, "Selma, we should paint a palm scenery on the balcony wall," and that was one time too many that Siegelchen suggested that.

Selma took the hot, very expensive porcelain coffee pot and threw it at the balcony wall and said, "There is your palm scenery," and from that moment on, the palm scenery was never mentioned again. Even today, writing the story, I smile.

In 1989, after the Berlin Wall came down that had divided East Berlin and West Berlin since 1948, we could freely travel into East Berlin. This was not possible before 1989, during the Russians' occupation and their restrictions. My mother took me to the streets where she grew up, and my mother was very tempted to go up to her childhood apartment, just to see whether the huge coffee stain was still on the balcony wall, because that balcony was never painted after it showed the coffee stain, which was there instead of the palm scenery. The very old photos that I still have are from my great-grandparents, and as I look at them, I can hear Selma speak those words about the palm scenery.

My mother grew up in a very loving and caring family, even though she was brought up by a nanny. She never met her father, who lived in Switzerland because he had tuberculosis and the mountain air was extremely healthy for him. Unfortunately he died during my grandmother's pregnancy with my mother.

My grandmother was forty-six years old when she had my mother. She had no idea that she was pregnant. She just kept complaining about not feeling well, which was unusual, because my grandmother was never sick, ever. Finally she saw a doctor, and to everybody's surprise she was told that she was pregnant. Obviously my mother was an only child.

Looking back and trying to put together the timeline, I think my grandmother must have had an affair with a blond, blue-eyed man while her husband lived for several years in Switzerland for tuberculosis treatment. Her husband had brown eyes and dark hair.

(This would later prove to be very helpful to my mother—something she could have never admitted to while my grandmother was still alive.)

My grandmother visited her husband often in Switzerland, but my mother would never admit to the affair. But truth be told, I think it is a good possibility, just by putting two and two together. My mother always said that a man like her father could get a woman pregnant till fifteen minutes before his death. *Really?* The man who impregnated my grandmother was an Aryan with blue eyes and blond hair. My mother would never accept this theory—the truth is something she took with her to her grave. She was totally against anybody writing about the Friedlaender or Hirsch families because she saw her birth as so shameful that she'd rather die than tell the truth. But the timeline is not too difficult to figure out. She would fight over this whole story of the Friedlaender and Hirsch families. So I am doing the best with what she told me, and the rest is what I actually experienced and saw. I found my grandfather's grave in 1990 in East Berlin, in the Jewish cemetery in Weissensee, and the gravestone read "Died 19th September 1918." My mother was born on May 2, 1919. My mother must have been a miraculous conception.

I can't think of a man who has sex on his mind after being deathly ill for many years. My grandfather begged his doctors to save his life, and he would have paid any amount of money to make that happen. But the doctors told him that there was nothing else they could do to save his life.

The Friedlaender and Hirsch family members all had brown eyes. My mother had blue eyes and strawberry blonde hair. (I had red hair and have green eyes.) Uncle Emil, my grandmother's brother, signed a document that stated that my grandmother had an affair and that my mother was the product of that affair, and that my mother's father was a non-Jew, which saved my mother's life before the Nazis almost shipped her off to a concentration camp. It was meant to be a fake document, not a government document. I believe that it actually was a true statement. I will never truly know, but I will always think that my mother was hiding her true father's identity, and it is possible that my grandmother withheld the truth from my mother out of shame or decency and my mother just put it all together but never really accepted it. Who knows?

My mother was born into a wealthy family and was spoiled. Her mother made sure that my mother grew up within the large Friedlaender clan with lots of uncles and cousins and nephews. They all came together regularly and most importantly on Jewish holidays. They had a lot of love for each other and celebrated a rich family life.

As a young teen she became a member of the Jewish Sport Club Maccabi and rowed for that club for several years. Her first marriage was to a Jewish man named Kramer, but the marriage only lasted six months and was annulled, since she was only eighteen when she married Mr. Kramer.

My grandfather was very wealthy due to the inheritance from his father, who built a business and created a fortune as a hatmaker in Breslau. They moved to Berlin and also moved the business. Before my mother passed, she told me that some lady told her that she was in Breslau and that there was a shingle at the hatmaker's shop, which was not occupied, that still had my great-grandfather's name on it. Hirsch Hat Maker was the name of the shop. That information was given to my mother around the year 2000-something, which made my mother very happy, even though she never met that side of her family. The image that she had in her head came from her mother telling her about her father. My mother loved that piece of information, which confirmed the history of her father's family.

My grandmother always said she would never depend on a man to make a living even if she got married. She said that before the turn of the twentieth century. She was very progressive for a woman at that time, when women stayed home and cooked, baked, cleaned the house, and took care of the children. Well, not my grandmother. She did not live by those rules.

My grandfather gave her a yearly allowance of 20,000 gold marks, which would today be approximately close to 325,000 dollars. This was the amount that he thought was needed to run the household—it was never used for my grandmother's business, ever. They never talked about money; he just filled up her account every so often, so the household would be running smoothly, even after he moved to the Swiss Alps for medical reasons.

My grandmother had a live-in maid and a nanny for my mother. She put all her energy into her business, which didn't leave her much time for a baby.

He had always wanted children and gave extravagant parties for children of his wife's family. He was extremely generous and spoiled his wife, my grandmother, in excess. According to my mother, he bought her very expensive jewelry, furs, and anything else she wanted or he thought she should have.

Her older brother, Emil, slowly but surely stole some of the jewelry to cover his debt for playing the horse track. He was addicted to gambling, only then it was not known as an addiction. My grandmother gave him a lot of money to cover his bets, but the stealing was something she could not forgive him for, because her husband would ask her about a certain piece of jewelry that he had bought for her and my grandmother would find an excuse for why she could not wear it. Her brother had a very successful bakery business that he put into jeopardy and eventually lost. He had a true talent to create those wonderful cakes that he became famous for, and then he lost it all because of his gambling. His bakery also did not survive because of the collapse of the market in 1929. Emil was definitely the

11

black sheep in the family and a very bad man because of what he did to me as I was growing up after World War II.

These stories told to me by my mother created my only experience of family.

Through her stories I feel that I knew all of them very well. I have these very old-fashioned photos and I can identify each person in these photos. When Hitler the dictator came to power, he stole my family by killing them one by one. One of my family members was Magda Friedlaender, later known as Mrs. Magda Goebbels. Following is the true historic account of Magda Friedlaender Goebbels, as my mother told me and as history confirmed it in videos shown by German television, where I saw it originally.

Before I tell the story of Magda Friedlaender Goebbels, it is important to understand what was happening in Europe under Hitler's Nazi regime.

# 1901–1945:
# The Magda Goebbels Story and the Nazis

When Hitler came to power in 1931, he immediately started to implement the plan that he had written about in his book, *Mein Kampf*, while he was imprisoned, giving rise to the Nazi rule in Germany. He enthralled the crowds with his hate speeches against the Jews. He introduced the practice of ethnic cleansing by selecting tall, blue-eyed, blond-haired men, committed to Hitler's ideology, and permitting them to have more than one wife at the same time. The wives, too, were "pure Aryans." The newborn babies of these women, who got impregnated on purpose, were taken from their mothers right after birth and handed over to the state to be trained from infanthood on, raised to be perfect Nazis and eventually die for the Fuehrer. There were more than 14,000 babies born between 1931 and 1940 that were raised in special schools to create the perfect Aryan Nazi. No mental or physical imperfections were permitted, especially not impurity of religion.

Hitler's idea was to get rid of the "imperfect humans," the Jews, in any way possible. He knew he would need help for such an enormous task.

At that time there were around 65,000 Jews living in Germany alone, not counting the Jews living in the rest of Europe, but Hitler did not want to eliminate just the Jews in Germany but also those in all of Europe, including Russia, as well as those in Egypt. He had the backing of Japan, which became his ally, and Mussolini, the dictator of Italy. He soon found many like-minded men and women who helped him in his murderous plan. The people that helped him were Dr. Joseph Goebbels, Heinrich Himmler, Herrmann Goering, Rudolph Hess, Adolf Eichmann, Martin Bormann, his personal architect Albert Speer, Mr. Ehrhardt, whose nickname was "Concentration-Camp Ehrhardt, and Dr. Mengele, whose nickname was "Butcher of Auschwitz," just to name a few. All these men who were close to Hitler would help him create and execute a plan for the systematic killing of Jews once and for all, and possibly worldwide. These men would be at Hitler's side, acting in his name, until the final days of the Third Reich and until the Jews, which he called "the unclean race," were eliminated. He also concentrated on the homosexuals, the mentally ill, Catholics, communists, gypsies, socialists, and union leaders.

Hitler created the *Schutzstaffel* (SS), which means "Protection Squadron" or "Defense Corps," but which was actually the Nazi version of the secret police. He also created the Gestapo, short for Geheime Staatspolizei, which means "Secret State Police." These were the official secret police—a group even more powerful and secretive than the SS and more powerful than military generals. The Gestapo could even arrest an SS officer or any high-ranking soldier as high up as a general if it suspected that person of not being a strict enough Nazi, not following the führer's orders or his ideology. Anyone who did not follow the führer's orders or ideology would easily wind up in a concentration camp or just hanged publicly, to demonstrate Hitler's power.

There were forty-six attempts by high-ranking military officers, including generals, who wanted to assassinate him: when found out, they were hanged publicly with very thin cable-like ropes chosen to make them suffer as long as possible, to make them die slowly. Please realize I am talking strictly high-ranking military, which meant military officers, who were soldiers, not policy makers. They saw the coming of the tragedy of this unnecessary war. They quickly saw that Hitler was insane. The first attempt at an assassination was done in Berlin by a young French civilian, who almost succeeded, almost. He was caught and not even tried; they just hanged him.

Baron von Staufenberg was probably the most famous officer who tried to eliminate Hitler, but there were many others, including the general who went by the nickname "Desert Fox," General Manfred Rommel, who fought Patton in North Africa and lost in 1944. Hitler was not happy and ordered Rommel to return to Berlin under house arrest. He sent a high-ranking Gestapo man to the house where Rommel lived with his wife and only son. The Gestapo told General Manfred Rommel that he had two choices, and both were instant death.

The options were 1) to be hanged publicly as a traitor and lose all the privileges his family would otherwise get, or 2) to bite on a cyanide capsule right there and then, get a state funeral and all the financial privileges for his family, and die a hero. Rommel was never a Nazi—he was strictly a military man and despised the Nazis. Rommel chose option two. He did not want his family to suffer and made that decision for their sake. He took the poison. His family was safe, and he did get a state funeral as a fallen high-ranking soldier and hero.

Albert Speer, as the head architect of the Third Reich, was responsible for building the concentration camps and the super-safe bunkers in Bavaria (which is called the "Eagle's Nest" and is part of the tour of the Bavarian Alps) and Berlin, where Hitler was hiding when needed. He created the concentration camp Dachau, on the outskirts of Munich, which served as a model for all other concentration camps.

It had wooden barracks that each would house up to one hundred people, though often many more would be forced into them. The barracks were built with very thin wooden panels that did not provide warmth in the winter or cooling in the summer heat. The bunks were stacked in three tiers made of wooden boards covered with very thin "mattresses," which passed for beds. The distance between the bunk tiers did not allow room to sit up.

There were many such camps built to achieve Hitler's Final Solution to the "Jewish problem." The "solution" was to kill as many Jews as possible through starvation, forced hard labor, execution-style killings, medical and science experiments, and gas chambers for mass killings. Huge deep graves were dug by the Jewish victims, who were then lined up at the very edge of the huge deep ditch that they just had dug and were shot in the head by SS who stood behind them. Sometimes the shooter missed, but the victim still fell into the ditch. If a fallen victim still moved, the victim was shot again. Many of these victims were still not dead and other victims just fell on top of them.

These mass graves were found when the camps were liberated in mid-April of 1945. The Nazis had succeeded in murdering a staggering six million Jews, plus four million non-Jews, whose crime was to have helped Jews by hiding them, or who exhibited physical imperfections, like having only one arm or leg, which they had most likely lost in World War I in the years 1914–1918, fighting for their fatherland, Germany. Homosexuals, people who had mental illnesses, and Catholics were also on the list of the killed.

This historical background is intended to provide context for the historical account of the life of Magda Goebbels. I write this as a part of history because Magda was a Friedlaender and was part of my family. We are Jews.

# The History of Magda Behrend, Friedlaender, Quandt, Goebbels

M agda was born in 1901 to Auguste Behrend. Her father was an engineer named Oskar Rietchel, a military man who wanted nothing to do with the child. Auguste worked as a servant for a wealthy Jewish family. It was there that Ms. Behrend met my great-uncle, Richard Friedlaender, who was the youngest of my grandmother's four brothers. When Magda, whose full name was Johanna Maria Magdalena, was three years old, my great-uncle Richard met and married Ms. Behrend and adopted Magda as his own daughter. She was raised in a religious Jewish home, and when she was about seven years old, she was given a necklace to wear that had a Star of David attached to it. My family had close ties with one another and got together almost weekly in addition to on birthdays and holidays. Those family gatherings would be held in various siblings' homes. They liked each other very much and were a close-knit family. Magda was always part of the family, just like the other children in the family—she was, after all, a member of the large Friedlaender clan.

She joined a Zionist organization, where she met a young boy named Chaim Arlossoroff, and they became very good friends. When she became a teenager, she was sent to a Belgian boarding school. There she learned etiquette and several languages, which would prove very useful to her later in life.

Members of my family were wealthy in their own right, and they all had their own businesses. It was not old money but the accomplishment of each of the Friedlaenders. Uncle Emil was a master baker, the only one that followed in his father's footsteps, and he had his own bakery and cake shop. His main problems were gambling and women. Later in life Emil married a Catholic prostitute named Mitze in order not to be picked up by the SS, thereby saving his own life. All Germans had to have a picture ID with them at all times, confirming their address and their religion. Soon all Jews had to wear the yellow Star of David with the word *Jude* ("Jew") fastened on their outer clothing.

Uncle Max was a banker; Uncle Albert imported and exported fine sherry and caviar and other delicacies. Their sister, Else, had already died in childbirth; the baby also died. Jenny, my grandmother, built a tobacco company and got rich in her own right. The

Greek connection will be featured later in my mother's life.

Richard Friedlaender was in commodities and could afford to give Magda the best of educations. Magda was very bright and pretty and was much liked. Magda loved children and was very good with them. When my mother was a child, she loved Magda. My mother used to tell me how special it was for her when Magda played with her.

At age eighteen, Magda returned from her boarding school in Belgium to Berlin. She was a real beauty, tall, with long blond hair and blue eyes. She was a statuesque young lady, and she turned the heads of men. She was still friends with Chaim Arlossoroff, and both were members of a Zionist organization. As Chaim grew older, he fell in love with Magda, and they talked about immigrating to Palestine together when the time was right.

Chaim Arlossoroff (whose hometown was Berlin) had already immigrated to British-occupied Palestine, where he was very active in the Zionist movement and became the first foreign minister. Meanwhile, Magda met the wealthy, much older industrialist Guenther Quandt, who fell in love with her, and he asked her to marry him. Though he was so much older and had been married previously and had adult children, Magda was impressed by his wealth and what he could offer her. When Magda was twenty years old, she married Guenther Quandt.

He had a huge villa in Grunewald, in the outskirts of Berlin, which still today is an exclusive neighborhood for the lifestyle of the rich and famous. My family visited Magda often at their villa. Soon Magda bore Quandt a son she named Harald. Of course Magda had house servants and a nanny and was spoiled rotten by her husband. Yet somehow, this was not enough for her. Since her husband traveled a lot, she became bored and lonely and began looking for ways to occupy her days. Out of boredom she went to one of Joseph Goebbels's speeches.

Dr. Joseph Goebbels was Reich minister of propaganda from 1933 to 1945. He was one of Hitler's devoted henchmen, known for his public speaking skills, his thorough anti-Semitism, and his advocacy of increasingly harsh policies against Jews. His speeches spoke of ways to humiliate the Jews and cleanse Germany of them. He called Jews *Judenschwein* (Jewish pigs) and *Schweinehunden* (pig-dogs), the lowest and most insulting cuss words in the German language. Amazingly Magda was impressed with his persona.

One day she went to Goebbels's office in the Reichskanzlei, or Reich Chancellery, where Hitler and his Waffen-SS and other high-ranking Nazis had their offices, even before Hitler was elected chancellor of Germany in 1931. Magda was so impressed that she decided to ask for a volunteer position, and she was given a job in Goebbels's office. She was immediately wonderstruck and smitten with him, and he was in awe of her beauty. That is how Magda Friedlaender Quandt and Dr. Joseph Goebbels, the Nazi propaganda and culture minister, met.

–

THEY SOON BECAME VERY PERsonal friends and admitted to loving each other. Joseph Goebbels told her that he wanted to marry her but that there were strings attached. One was divorcing Quandt, which was no problem for her, since she did not really love him. She just loved the life he could provide for her. The other was to rid herself of anything Jewish in her life. That meant separating herself from her stepfather and the rest of the family. She indeed divorced Quandt. Despite Mr. Quandt's knowledge of why she was divorcing him, he bought Magda an expensive apartment in a very exclusive and nice area in the center of Berlin and paid her a monthly allowance of 5,000 reichsmarks, which at that time was a lot of money. She also took her son Harald with her.

Since Goebbels at that time had only a modest salary and a small per diem, it was very convenient for him that Magda had a nice big apartment. Magda, who was raised as a Jew, married Dr. Joseph Goebbels, the Nazi minister of propaganda, in December of 1931. But before that, without blinking an eye, she denounced her upbringing and removed herself from anything that could be suspicious about her Jewish upbringing or any connection to the Jewish family that had given her a good home and elite schooling to help her to become a sophisticated lady. None other than Adolf Hitler himself, the newly elected chancellor of Germany, was the best man at their wedding. The photos of Dr. and Mrs. Goebbels were displayed in business windows and other public places. Hitler was not married, having only a mistress (the starlet Eva Braun), and this fact made Magda Goebbels the First Lady of Germany. Magda's good looks and education were very useful to the Nazis, especially during official visits from foreign heads of states, where her ability to speak multiple languages came in very handy.

German women were crazy about Magda, copying the way she dressed and the way she wore her beautiful, long blond hair, which she braided around her head until it almost looked like a crown. She represented her husband, Hitler, and the Third Reich very well.

She was seen with the children of the Hitler Youth and at many receptions; wherever she showed up, she received flowers and applause. Everywhere she went she was surrounded by throngs of people—arms outstretched—hoping for the chance to shake her hand. She must have truly felt that she had it all, that her life was perfect, or at least that's how it seemed. One would think that, but it all was a facade, except her ideology of the Third Reich, which was getting rid of the Jews.

Meanwhile, maybe a year after Magda's wedding to Goebbels, Chaim Arlossoroff, her childhood friend and sweetheart, returned to Berlin from Palestine, being on a mission to connect with Berliner Jews.

The British government still occupied Palestine and did everything possible to prevent Jews from migrating to Palestine. Ships carrying Jews and later survivors of the Holocaust were ordered to turn around and go elsewhere. The most famous ship not being allowed to enter Palestine was the *Exodus*. Leon Uris wrote a book about this true happening, and later it was made into a movie (with the actor Paul Newman as the leader of the people that lived on the ship).

Those who managed to survive the camps and migrate to Palestine were treated harshly by the British military. They were put into barbed wire camps, still wearing the striped pajama-like outfits they wore at the concentration camp. The occupation would not end until 1948, when the United Nations declared Palestine a sovereign state, which was called, from that moment on, the State of Israel. But when Chaim came to Berlin in the midthirties from what was still British-occupied Palestine, his mission was to get money for Palestine. He wanted to encourage Jews to give money for the Jewish cause in Palestine and to urge them to emigrate.

Upon arriving in Berlin, he was astonished to see "his" Magda in one of the photos that were displayed around town—with her husband Joseph Goebbels. He contacted Magda's half sister Arianna Schepard (Magda's mother's child from another relationship), who advised him to leave Berlin immediately, as his life was in danger. He followed her advice and returned to British-occupied Palestine in shock. Shortly after his return, he took a walk on the beach of Tel Aviv. He was approached by two men, who asked him if he was Chaim Arlossoroff, and he confirmed that he was. The men shot Arlossoroff and disappeared into the night. Chaim Arlossoroff, the first foreign minister to Palestine, bled out and died on the beach of Tel Aviv. The assassins were never found, and the British did not make any effort to find them. However, many believed that the assassins were Germans and most likely were sent by Goebbels because of his connection to Magda. Today every city in Israel has a street that is named Chaim Arlossoroff Street.

Magda bore Goebbels three girls in a row. He is known to have said to her that the next child had better be a boy, as if the gender of the children had been her choice. However, their next child was indeed a male, the only boy she had with Goebbels.

Despite giving Goebbels a son, and despite her good looks, Magda soon found out that her husband was having affairs, mostly with young starlets. If the woman declined his advances, he would shut down the production of the film she was making. It was well within his power as the minister of propaganda to decide which movie was to be made and which was not. Magda eventually went to Hitler to complain about her husband's affairs, and he intervened; this was the one and only time that the führer got involved in a marital affair. He spoke with Goebbels about the matter. Goebbels did not stop but became more secretive. He certainly did not want the führer's wrath on his head. Magda and Goebbels had two more children, making a total of six. All of her children's first names began with the letter H. Harald, her son from her marriage to Guenther Quandt, was enlisted into the SS at age fourteen at Magda's request. Members of my family have told my mother that this was against Harald's will. Harald

Quandt would survive the war and become the owner of Bavarian Motor Works, better known as BMW, the company that makes the famous cars. He died in his fifties after crashing an airplane he was piloting. Magda's perfect life seems not to have been as perfect after all. Over the years there was an obvious change in Magda's face. It turned from very pretty to jealous. Toward the end of her life, she became very bitter, and this bitterness distorted her facial appearance.

In 1938 Magda's stepfather, Richard Friedlaender (my great-uncle), had bought passage to America but needed Goebbels's permission to leave Germany to immigrate to the United States. When Richard Friedlaender showed up at Goebbels's office, Goebbels said to his adjutant, "Ask the Jew Friedlaender what he wants from me." So it was no surprise that Richard did not get the permission needed to leave the country. Instead, the opposite happened. A few days after the meeting with Goebbels, Richard Friedlaender was one of the first two thousand Berliner Jews to be picked up for transportation to a concentration camp. The Gestapo took them to the Buchenwald concentration camp, where my great-uncle died six months after his arrival. Supposedly his death was the result of a heart attack. In truth he died because of the hard labor that was demanded of the Jews in Buchenwald, and in all concentration camps, and because he did not get enough nourishment; he was hungry and dehydrated. (I have a video that shows him signing in at the concentration camp in Buchenwald at the time of his arrival there. We know so much about the concentration camps because the Nazis were keeping exact records and a register of everybody inside the camps and of everything that happened. Also the American generals Ike Eisenhower and General Patton, when they entered Germany in 1945, gave an order to register and photograph everything the way it was when they first entered the first concentration camp. Their efforts made it possible to show proof of the horrendous slaughter that the Nazis created and were guilty of.)

Richard Friedlaender died in the Buchenwald concentration camp after six months of hard labor, one of the first of some six million Jews the Nazis killed in camps before their reign of madness would be put to an end. Four million additional non-Jews plus the six million Jews were murdered, totaling ten million innocent lives that died in gas chambers, mass killings, the damned ovens, from dehydration and starvation and freezing to death. However, the story of what happened after Richard's murder is quite unusual.

A sealed coffin, supposedly containing the remains of my great-uncle, was sent from the Buchenwald concentration camp back to Berlin, to the Jewish cemetery in Weissensee, for a traditional Jewish burial. It was the most remarkable thing—that a murdered Jew who died in a concentration camp would be shipped back to his hometown for a proper Jewish burial. There are two theories as to how this came about.

The first is that Magda Goebbels asked her husband for this last favor, the smallest gesture of dignity for her stepfather, and that he agreed.

The second is that Magda enlisted help from others around her and kept it a secret from her husband. Given that Joseph Goebbels was so anti-Semitic, I think the second scenario seems more likely.

In any case, Jews were killed by the millions during these years, and their bodies were either thrown into mass graves or shoved into those damned ovens in the camps, or they died in gas chambers. The fact that this one particular Jew was returned to Berlin, his hometown, in a coffin, to receive a traditional Jewish burial, is almost impossible to believe. But my mother, who was nineteen years old at the time, was at the funeral and remembered all the details of the burial. Richard's siblings and their families were there, except for Albert, who lived in Egypt, where he had two hotels. The SS and German soldiers were watching the proceedings.

The coffin was sealed and could not be opened to verify what was actually in it.

Why was the SS there? What were they afraid of?

Was the coffin filled with rocks to make it seem that there was body inside? That is what my family thought, that the coffin did not contain Richard's body.

Since my mother was nineteen years old at the time when this took place and told me that she recalled the event quite well, even so many years later, I believe what she told me. She never wanted this story to get out, and I had to wait till after her death to tell this story, because I think it is a very important story and the world should know it.

My mother and I visited the Jewish cemetery in Weissensee in 1990, after the fall of the Berlin Wall in 1989. We indeed found the grave of Richard Friedlaender, as well as that of Else Stolzmann, my grandmother's younger sister, and her stillborn baby. Else was always afraid of the dark and always said she never wanted to be buried in a coffin alone; unfortunately her naive wish as a young woman was fulfilled in the most morbid way. The baby and she died during childbirth, and that is why it was possible to bury them together in the same coffin.

Toward the end of April in 1945, at the end of the Third Reich, Magda and Joseph Goebbels moved into the bunker in Berlin where Hitler and his concubine, Eva Braun, were already living.

The Russians were closing in from the east, preparing to enter Berlin. They were very eager to get to Hitler, hoping to capture him alive. Despite the viciousness of the German war machine, the war was finally over, but lost. The Third Reich lay in ruins, and so did hundreds of German cities. Millions of innocent people had died. The cowardly Hitler wanted to escape a jury and chose suicide instead. He gave his personnel that lived in the bunker explicit instructions not to let his body fall into enemy hands. First, Hitler killed his beloved dog, a German shepherd named Blondi who was Hitler's constant companion. Hitler married Eva Braun one day before taking the lives of himself and Eva, now Mrs. Hitler. Eva Hitler bit on a cyanide capsule; Hitler simultaneously bit on a capsule and shot himself. The staff in the bunker dragged the corpses into the courtyard, doused them with gasoline, and set them on fire, just as the führer had instructed, and put them into a shallow grave.

The entire Goebbels clan was also in the bunker. Two days after the Hitlers killed themselves, the Goebbelses killed their six children by feeding them poisoned chocolate. Harald Quandt, Magda's son from her marriage to Guenther Quandt, was not in the bunker with them. He was still a "good" Nazi fighting for the Thousand-Year Reich. I say "good" because he never wanted to be a Nazi; in fact, he expressed that to the family. He was, after all, only fourteen years old when he was forced to enlist. He only enlisted to please his mother. The other reason, which I am happy about, that he was not in the bunker is that his mother would have poisoned him as well, as she did her other six children.

The staff had not been ordered to be killed or take poison, as the so-called leaders did. After Magda poisoned her six children, the Goebbelses returned to their private quarters and played cards. Magda was heard to say to the staff, "If my children cannot grow up in the Third Reich, then they shall not live at all." The Goebbelses committed their own suicides by taking cyanide pills the next day, and they were also doused with gasoline and set on fire in the courtyard of the bunker and put into shallow graves. Here was a woman who had it all: beauty, the trust of the führer, the status as First Lady of the land, money, servants, beautiful children, prestige, and she killed it all for her belief in the Third Reich and its political, racist, murderous attitude.

When the Russians stormed the bunker, they found the bodies of the six Goebbels children laid out in their white nightgowns next to each other in the courtyard, from the littlest to the oldest, just like organ pipes.

This true account of Magda Goebbels's story was partially told to me by my mother; parts have also been told in published books and produced on film by German historians. I have a video that German historians produced and that the German government documented and aired in Germany. My mother bought a copy for me from the TV station that aired Magda's story.

Berlin was the most sought-after city to ruin and destroy by the Allies. It was a frightening sight, but we were lucky, we were alive, and even though the front of the building was destroyed during one of the Allied bombings, the back of the building where we lived was still intact. I did not understand the danger very well. All that was known to me was war, which is something no child or anybody should have to experience. I didn't know life to be any other way, and therefore I was not as afraid as people may think. The fear in me only happened much later, when I started going to school and people talked about the war and asked my mother questions about the war and how we survived (being Jewish was a fact we were still trying to hide), which really did not mean anything to me at the time. The answers my mother gave were more explanatory, and that's when I started to understand the danger we had been in. I also was a little older and understood more.

One year in a lifetime of a child can make a whole lot of difference in being able to comprehend and understand. I also was afraid of any change. Those changes for a little girl can literally affect your life and are not easy to handle. Till today I can recall my fears and apprehension of any kind of change, whether it was a new place or people I had never met before. I still am afraid to live in a single free standing house.

# Final Consequences for
# Hitler's Other Collaborators

Goehring, the war minister, was hiding in a big farmhouse outside of Berlin, but he was finally found by the Allies. They pretended to be from the press, and they supposedly wanted to interview him and have him sign some documents. Goehring always believed that he would be the next chancellor of Germany—he was known for his cockiness and the fancy uniforms he wore and the golden staff he always held in his hand. When Goehring stepped out of his house, he saw the uniformed Allies sitting at a table in front of the building where he lived. Soon he became aware that they were there to arrest him. His uniform with all its medals and the staff were taken from him by the Allies, the Americans, French, and British. He was taken to Nuremberg and imprisoned in order to await the Tribunal for Crimes against Humanity.

All prisoners were watched closely, the guards checking the cells every fifteen minutes through a small spyglass in each door. Goehring used an ointment for his inner thighs, which were infected (his weight caused his thighs to rub against each other, and that's what caused the infection). Every day, he asked the guards for his medical ointment, which was brought to him, and he was supervised by the guard as he applied it. Then the guard would reconfiscate the jar of ointment when leaving his cell. Unbeknownst to the guards, Goehring had shrewdly hidden a cyanide capsule in the ointment. When he realized that he would not escape the tribunals for crimes against humanity and would be sentenced to death, Goehring took that cyanide capsule. He, unfortunately, cheated the hangman, like so many other high-ranking Nazis.

Rudolph Hess, Hitler's ace pilot, was sentenced to life in Spandau Prison in Berlin. He died there of old age. Heinrich Himmler, who was responsible for the extermination of the Jews, was captured by the British, who thought he was a German soldier, and was kept in a POW camp. He had shaved off his mustache and changed his hairstyle, so he was not easily recognizable. Eventually somebody realized who this POW really was. The British military arrested him, and he became a political enemy prisoner to stand trial at the Nuremberg Tribunals for Crimes against Humanity. However, he also had a cyanide capsule hidden in one of his teeth, which he bit down on when he realized that the British knew who he really was. He, as well, cheated the hangman.

The Allied military wanted the men who were responsible for millions of Jewish and other people's deaths tried by Allied judges. The judges tried very hard to bring them to trial, and many of them took their own lives before they could be tried. Dr. Mengele, the concentration camp physician in Auschwitz, used prisoners as human guinea pigs for medical procedures without anesthesia. Hundreds of them died slowly and in agony—worse than being killed in the gas chambers. Some, who survived and lived to tell about their ordeal, were maimed for life, either physically or emotionally. He disappeared somewhere in South America; it was said he was in the jungle somewhere in Brazil, but he was never found.

Eichmann, another of those high-ranking Nazis, responsible for killing almost a whole concentration camp, immigrated to Argentina. Israeli agents found him in 1959 and kidnapped him and brought him to Israel, where he was put on trial. Many Israelis who survived his extermination camp testified against him, and he was sentenced to death. After he was executed, his ashes were flown out over the Mediterranean, where they were disposed of. A lot of this is known, as told by survivors and by historians. There is a difference between a concentration camp and an extermination camp. The Jews that were sent to extermination camps were designated to be killed—that's why they called them extermination camps or death camps. These poor people were not given a chance to survive, as, for instance, labor camp prisoners. Many of those also died, but they had a slim chance of survival.

Eichmann's trial was broadcast live via radio, and Israelis listened to his testimony, walking around with transistor radios glued to their ears on the way to work or wherever they had to go. Television was not available at that time.

# My Family's Life in Nazi Times

n 1935, Jews started to prepare for the worst, as it was obvious that they would be hunted and killed—it was just a question of when. Some of my family tried to leave Germany, which was extremely difficult because they had to have permission from the government to do so or have enough money to pay smugglers to get them out of Germany. Jews paid a lot of money or bribes, many times with jewelry and other valuables that they had hidden from the Nazis.

The Nazis first confiscated all firearms and ammunition and then the bank accounts, including safety boxes. They would force entrance to Jewish-owned apartments or houses and take anything valuable, like valuable original paintings (of which some are still found to date in very strange places and in other countries), silver and gold cutlery, carpets, chandeliers, and of course jewelry, religious artifacts like Shabbat candle holders, prayer books bound with silver covers, and even furniture. Today I hear people say, "Why did the Jews not defend themselves?" Well, it was because the Nazis confiscated everything that they considered weapons, which included butcher knives from the kitchen. They started that in mid-1935 until they were sure that they had all the weapons confiscated. They wanted to prevent Jews from being able to fight back.

One of my great-cousins, Edith Stolzmann, married a man from Poland who lived in Berlin. They had a baby. The Nazis immediately declared the whole family Polish and discarded the German birth certificate of the baby and my cousin. As Poles they were not allowed to live in German (just like other non-Germans, who were deported or transported to concentration camps). They were picked up and transported to the Warsaw Ghetto in Poland, where thousands of Jews like my cousin and Polish Jews were held and watched by the German Nazis and Hitler's elite SS, the Leibwaffen Standarte.

Despite this surveillance, the Jews of the ghetto found ways to smuggle in weapons, ammunition, and food (they were only given rations of minimal amounts of food, not enough to survive). One of the main ways that things were smuggled into the ghetto was by children crawling through sewer and water pipes to sneak outside the ghetto walls. We know that when the Nazis found out that Jews in the ghetto had organized a militia, the ghetto was stormed by the Nazis, and all the people in that ghetto, which was a walled-in town, were ordered to come out of their homes and face the wall that surrounded the ghetto. They then were shot, one by one, the Germans not caring if they were children or babies. My cousin, her husband, and their baby were among the dead. Nobody who lived in the Warsaw ghetto survived that killing.

After the Kristallnacht (crystal night) of September 1939, when Jewish stores were boycotted and destroyed, the display windows painted with white Stars of David and with writing saying "don't buy Jewish" and "out with the Jews," and synagogues set on fire, there was a definite knowledge among the Jews of what was to come. Jews scrambled to leave Germany, and a few thousand succeeded. Many of them found their way to Palestine, despite the British prohibitions. Others went to other countries like Argentina or the United States. If the Jews had just moved to another European country, they still would have suffered the same danger of being picked up and sent to concentration camps.

–

MEANWHILE, SINCE MY GRAND-mother had contacts at the Greek embassy, since she employed Greek citizens in her tobacco business, she made arrangements with the Greek embassy for a possible getaway from Berlin to Greece. She and my mother studied Greek and even changed their first names to Greek names, and they hid their valuables by sewing them into the hems of coats and jackets and finding hiding places for money, since the bank accounts were confiscated by the Nazis. Many Jews did that, using those valuables for payoffs to people who would or could help them.

# My Father's Story

Yanis Liniratos was the air attaché for the Greek embassy to Berlin, the capital of Germany. He came from the city of Salonika, Greece, where he grew up in a large family, and all male members of his family were educated and schooled in a Greek military academy. They were wealthy because they owned vineyards. He met my mother through my grandmother, in Berlin, where he was assigned to by the Greek Royal Palace to serve as an air attaché at the Greek embassy. My grandmother hired Greeks because they had great knowledge of tobacco, which was her business. She had a tobacco factory and sold her products under the name NIL, the German spelling for the Egyptian river Nile.

Air Attaché Liniratos met my mother at one of the embassy's functions, and soon they had an affair. Yanis offered to marry my mother in 1939, when the situation for the Jews was already deadly. He wanted to save her from the Nazis and take her to Greece to also save her from World War II. My grandmother was very ill in a hospital. When my mother asked her mother, who was in a hospital, whether it was ok with her if she went with Yanis to Greece, my grandmother made my mother feel guilty by saying, "If you can leave your dying mother here knowing you will never see her again, then go with God, but go." There is this "Jewish guilt" thing that is passed on from female to female through generations, and every Jewish female has it; it is genetic.

After the Kristallnacht, when the Jewish stores were destroyed and their showcase windows were broken (hence the term "crystal night," or the night of the broken glass), Yanis was deported by the Nazis and had to leave Germany within twenty-four hours. My mother did not know at that time that she was pregnant with me. The fact that he was an embassy employee did not stop the Nazis from deporting him and all foreigners; no embassy could save any of them. They either left within twenty-four hours or would be transported to a concentration camp.

As it turned out, when the Germans overran Greece in 1941, just as they did with most of Europe, they hunted the Greek opposition and killed those people, including 60,000 Jews from Salonika. They found my father and shot him during that occupation of Greece in 1941. Therefore, somehow, with all the difficulty ahead of us, it was good for my mother not to have gone to Greece. I do not know a lot about my father, just that he was born in Salonika to a wealthy vineyard family and that he was attractive and extremely punctual. He was small in stature and had blue eyes and reddish-brown hair (for a Greek, very unusual). I have green eyes and red hair, possibly something I got from my Greek father. I never even saw a picture of him.

# My Story

I was born in May of 1940 in the only Jewish hospital in Berlin. The Nazis immediately made sure that I was identified as a Jew by forcing my mother to choose a Jewish first name for me from a list of nine girls' names, just as Jewish boys were named from a list of boys' names. My mother chose the name Tana with the last name Hirsch, both being Jewish. My grandmother passed away three months after my birth. My mother lived with a Jewish family by the name of Storm. She was forced into a labor camp six weeks after I was born, where she helped make weapons for the German war machine.

The Storm family took care of me until the beginning of 1943, when my mother was released from the labor camp. Soon, also in early 1943, the Storms were picked up by the SS. Thankfully my mother had met a German soldier in early 1943 who wanted to help. His name was Arthur Glyz, and he was an Aryan. Even though he knew my mother was Jewish because she wore the yellow Star of David with the word *Jude* ("Jew") written on it, he wanted to help. (All Jews were

No. I

E 2

# Geburtsurkunde

(Standesamt Berlin-Wedding .................................................. Nr. 3079

Tana Hirsch — — — — — — — — — — — — — — — — —

ist am 28.Mai 1940 — — — — — — — — — — — — — — — —

in Berlin, im Krankenhause der jüdischen Gemeinde, — — — — — — geboren

Mutter: Kontoristin Else Sara Hirsch — — — — — — — — —

— — — — — — — — griechisch-orthodox, früher mosaisch, — — —

Änderungen der Eintragung: — — — — — — — — — — — — —

....................................................................................

....................................................................................

....................................................................................

.............. Berlin .................., den .... 28.Mai ........................ 19 40.

## Der Standesbeamte

In Vertretung: ..............................

(Siegel)

48

required to wear that yellow star, which was to be worn at all times). He made it possible for me to be taken away from the Storm family before they were picked up (my mother had no clue that they would be picked up), and he took me to a Christian family outside Berlin who did not know my religion or where I came from. He just explained to them that Berlin was too dangerous for a child and that's why he brought me to them, which was very understandable to them.

When the Storms were picked up, my mother was in the building. That day, fortunately, she did not wear the yellow Star of David, even though not wearing the star was punishable by death. As she was walking up the stairs to visit the family Storm, she heard the SS with their heavy boots coming up behind her. She was asked where she was going. Somehow, she remembered a random name of someone who lived in that building. She told them that name, and she was told to leave the building immediately. Standing in the street on the sidewalk, she saw Mr. and Mrs. Storm being yanked out of their apartment and taken to trucks waiting in the street. Mr. Storm was put on one truck and Mrs. Storm was put on a different truck. They were calling each other's names, and then the trucks took off. Nobody knows where to, but my mother never heard from or saw the Storm family again.

My mother was in total shock. Just imagine what would have happened if she had worn the yellow Star of David She would have been put into one of those trucks, and it would have transported her to a concentration camp. A few weeks later, she received a letter from the SS that ordered her to report to a collection place at a certain date with hundreds of other Jews, all from Berlin. She had in her hand the document, created by an SS doctor, that explained that her mother, my grandmother, had had an affair with a man of Aryan decent and therefore my mother should be considered a half Jew. The term "half Jew" was coined by Hitler and Goebbels, who declared that a child of a mixed-religious Jew-and-Christian marriage with an Aryan man or woman could be considered a half Jew (which does not truly exist. In the Jewish religion, you can only be a Jew if your mother is Jewish, so either you are a Jew or you are not). These "half Jews" had to pass a physical test that measured their body parts according to the SS idea of Aryan purity. The test was given by an SS doctor, who examined and measured the nose, ears, eyes and their color, natural hair color, forehead, neck, height and general physical appearance. She was declared a half Jew. Here is the place were my grandmothers affair saved her daughters life (my mother's life).

With this SS doctor's document in hand, my mother showed up at a collection center for transportation to a concentration camp. Instructions were that she was permitted to bring only one suitcase. The document that the SS doctor gave her confirming that she was a half Jew saved her life. She was allowed to leave and was warned that she still had to wear the yellow star and that she could be picked up at any time for transportation to a concentration camp. It was clear that the danger was not over for us. Under no circumstance could we let anybody know that we were Jewish—that still could have cost my mother's and my lives.

# My Mother's and My Lives During Nazi Time

M y mother went into hiding. She found a tiny furnished room in a large apartment in a central area of Berlin.

The house the German soldier took me to was owned by a nice elderly couple. The house had a big backyard for me to explore and play in. They had a dog, a German shepherd. The dog was a trained watchdog and would not let anybody in or out. Unless a command was given for him to let that person pass, he would bite a person with a hold like a vice grip and would not let go of the person until told by the owners to sit.

One afternoon the dog's owners were looking for me but could not find me. They would call my name, but there was no response until they called the dog by his name. He would come out of the doghouse with me attached to his back. It was kind of funny because when it came to me he was very gentle. The owners did not know that and feared that the dog would harm me.

One day I was playing in the yard and saw a silhouette against the setting sun. I was not sure what to make of it, but I thought that this was maybe my mother. My instinct told me not to call her, and she did not call me. Then, suddenly, the silhouette was gone. Later in life, when we were reunited, she told me that she was there; she just wanted to see me, but it was too dangerous to call my name.

The people that harbored me did not know that I was Jewish, which was good because their son was an SS officer, which I learned when he came home one day on leave. He demonstrated a gas mask, which was given only to high-ranking SS personnel because the Germans were afraid that the British were using gas bombs when bombing Germany. It was scary to see the mask on him. How ironic that a Jew was taken care of by people who were Nazis, and they did not know. I told my mother later when we were reunited about the strange uniform and the gas mask. It was too late to be concerned or afraid.

I did not know my mother until I was five years old. We had been hiding in separate places so as not to be found by the SS or Gestapo. Somehow, I was reunited with my mother in the last days of April 1945 in Berlin. According to my mother, her girlfriend Sophie, who was not Jewish, picked me up and took me to my mother. Sophie told me to call her "Mutti" (mother) in public so people would not wonder what she was doing with a child. It was during the last ten days of the war and the bombing of Berlin that my mother and lived together. Fear of the dark followed me from my childhood through my teenage years, even until now. Memories can be painful, very cruel and lingering, even when they happen to a very young child. I believe, today, that much of my personality has to do with what happened to me as a very young child. At times it was almost impossible to overcome myself because of memories that kept creeping up at the most difficult moments of my life. I remember being afraid a lot, and hungry. Later in my life throughout my life I have always overloaded my plate at mealtimes, knowing I would not be able to eat the amount that I put on my plate.

The British unleashed a twenty-four-hours-a-day bombing of German cities during the last ten days of the war. They concentrated on Berlin day and night. It was a most frightening experience. I remember some people, in between bombings, went to their apartments, returning to the cellar or bunker and sharing the food that they still had. My mother had taken off her yellow Star of David, so nobody knew that we were Jews. It was announced through the radio that Germany had capitulated and had lost the war. The bombing stopped on May 8, 1945, and then we were finally able to come out of the bunker and go to our small room, which was my mother's hiding place.

Of course, Berlin was burning and in total ruins just a little more than the rest of Germany because of Hitler's bunker.

It was a frightening sight, but we were lucky; we were alive, and even though the front of the building was destroyed during one of the Allied bombings, the back of the building, where we lived, was still intact. I did not really understand the danger very well. All I knew was war, which is something no child or anybody should have to experience. I did not know life to be any other way, and therefore I was not as afraid as people may think. The fear in me only happened much later, when I started school and people talked about the war and I noticed the sudden difference of no bombs or darkness. I did ask my mother questions about the war and how we survived. We still could not talk about being Jewish, and I still did not know that I was Jewish. The danger of Nazis in hiding that still killed Jews obviously existed, and so did the fear. My mother gave me explanatory answers to my questions, and that's when I started to understand the danger we were in. I also was a little older and understood more. One year in a lifetime of a child can make a whole lot of difference in being able to comprehend and understand. I also was afraid of change. Those changes for a little girl can be literally life changing and not easy to handle. I can recall my fears and apprehension of any kind of change, whether it was a new place or people I had never met before. Even today, I am afraid of the dark and of living in a single-standing dwelling. My fear is so strong that I would not move into a house my husband wanted to buy, so we always lived in apartments with walls that touched each other.

I was five years old, though my memory goes back further than that. I remember so many things, like the smell of burning flesh, the dead animals and people in the streets, and the constant darkness. There were very few good things to remember in the first place from my childhood through my teenage years and into adulthood.

In Germany, when you walked into an apartment, there was a long hallway, dimly lit, and on each side of the hallway there were doors that opened up into rooms. Our room was the last and smallest room at the end of a long, dark hallway. We had a couch that we shared for sleeping, two chairs, one table, and a closet.

The British knew that Hitler and other high-ranking Nazis were hiding in the impenetrable bunker, and that is why they bombed Berlin so vehemently. We heard the sirens, warning us of bomb attacks, going day

and night. It was a frightening time for a girl. We noticed when we went to the shelter that fewer and fewer
people showed up. Some of them were killed by a di-
rect hit of a bomb and others were killed from falling
debris and collapsing buildings. My foot was damaged
by falling debris from a building that collapsed. I still
have that scar.

The Russians were approaching Germany from the
east, and the Americans approached Germany from the
west. The Americans had already liberated France and
advanced into Germany from the west. They crossed
the Rhine River, clearing the western cities of Germany
and liberating the concentration camps as they moved
toward Berlin. The Russians were ready to enter Berlin
from the east, and the Americans agreed to that. This
was, as we learned later, a political blunder and a huge
mistake. If the Russians had not entered Berlin first,
then later, in 1948, when Germany was divided by the
Allies into East and West, there would not have been
the problem with East and West Germany, and Berlin
would never have been divided by the wall.

On May 8, 1945 it was announced that the war was
over and that Germany had lost. Germany was in ruins.
It seemed that not one house was standing, or at least
the buildings were in ruins. Germany had lost the war,
and the next chapter of life after the war began, which

was difficult and still dangerous, in particular for the Jews. The Russians stormed Hitler's bunker in order to find Hitler and his cohort, which they did, in a shallow grave in the courtyard of the bunker, which was built by architect Albert Speer, Hitler's private architect. They took Hitler's charred head, and one person transported it to Moscow. The hate that the Russians had against the Germans came from the fact that Hitler had signed a peace treaty with Stalin (the president of Russia), promising not to attack Stalingrad. Nevertheless, Hitler did attack Stalingrad, and a bitter fight ensued that cost more than twenty-two million lives. It was a waste of effort and a senseless loss of those precious lives, an idiotic political move that Hitler absolutely could not win.

When the Russians reached Germany, they created havoc in Germany, and a great deal happened in Berlin. Besides the Russians, we also were still surrounded by Nazis, who did not go away—they only went underground. The great danger was that the Nazis didn't wear uniforms anymore, and therefore you never knew who was and who was not a Nazi. It was a very dangerous situation. Those underground Nazis were known for their cruelty, and everybody feared them. By the same token, we were afraid of all the Allies, since we did not know what would happen. After all we were still the enemy. The Nazis that went into hiding caused misery and death to Jews. Those Nazis were called the Werewolves and still believed in the resurrection of the Third Reich, and they were deadly.

The German ex-soldiers took their uniforms off and burned them in the streets, in fear that the Russians might recognize them as German soldiers, because that meant being tortured and shot. The streets in Berlin and other cities were covered with burning uniforms. The Russians were cruel against the Germans, and they did not discriminate between men and women, young and old. The females, no matter their ages, were raped. The Russian army killed thousands of Germans by breaking into their apartments, plundering them of their belongings, dragging people out of the buildings, and torturing and then shooting them.

# Our Post-War Lives

One day I observed how the Russians treated a man who walked with a cane. They made him cross a channel at a partially destroyed bridge. The man was forced to walk on a wooden plank that the Russian soldiers placed from the bank to the part of the bridge that was still intact. He was old and his upper body bent over. After a few steps on the wooden plank, the man lost his footing and fell into the ice-cold water. The Russians were standing on the bank of the channel and laughed and shot bullets into the water. The man was never seen again.

The channel is located at the end of one of Berlin's largest parks, the Tiergarten. We stood there watching in disbelief and then were told by the Russians to leave. We had to cross through the park, which was far away from where we were living. My mother chose a shortcut, which was walking across the grassy area of the park, a felony under normal circumstances. We saw a line of Russians on either side of the park along the route we had to get to. My mother started to run, and I tried to keep up with her. We expected something bad to happen because we had Russians behind and in front of us. Fear did give us adrenaline (only we did not know that at that time) as we ran to the end of the park, where the Russian soldiers were standing with drawn weapons. This was the only way for us to get where we had to go. We just wanted to make it past the Russians, hoping they would not attack us or harm us in any way, because we had just seen what they were capable of doing.

We made it, and they just told us to keep running, away from them. After we reached the road, we turned to see what had happened and if anybody was following us. My mother saw a sign saying "MINEFIELD." Wow, did we really just cross a minefield? Did she not know? Only then did she realize the multiple dangers we were in. My mother explained to me what had just happened and how lucky we were not to have stepped on a mine and also to have survived the Russians behind and in front of us, with their rifles pointing at people walking by. I was blissfully ignorant, being five years old. But my mother realized the multiple dangers we were in. I started shaking and crying. I understood that we were in immediate danger. My mother told me to take a deep breath and pretend that everything was ok. Which it was! There is a German saying: "Fools and drunks and babies are the luckiest people." We were the fools, very lucky!

We had another experience with the Russians. One day, still in the beginning of May, we came home and saw a big hole in the entrance door, which was made of oak wood, of the apartment where we lived. It looked as if somebody had taken an axe to the door to open the entrance door from the inside. My mother signaled to me to be quiet and follow behind her. As we entered our room, we saw three Russians in uniform standing there. Just imagine the shock and fear that went through us at that time. We watched them turning everything upside down looking for valuables, which we did not have, because the Nazis took them. My mother told me to hide behind the couch and stay still. On the table we had in the room was a picture of my mother and the German soldier Arthur Glyz, the one that saved our lives during the Holocaust. The Russians were pointing to that picture, wanting to know where he was. My mother indicated that he had not come back yet. Then they opened the closet and pulling everything out, finding the yellow Star of David with the word *Jude* written on it.

They somehow understood that we were Jews. They picked me up and told my mother (who was still in fear) to come with them. We had no idea what would happen to us. They took us to their barracks, where they offered us food. They gave me a huge slice of white bread with real butter and a very tall glass of milk. To this day, I believe that that was the sweetest glass of milk I ever drank, and the bread tasted like cake. If they had not found out that we were Jews, there is no telling what they might have done to us. The Russians also, just like all the Allies, helped free the concentration camp survivors. There is no doubt in my mind that these Russians saved our lives.

They offered housing to my mother, me, and my mother's friend Sophie at their quarters because they thought it was not safe enough to live in the city due to warlike outbreaks, partially by the Russians. They were very good to us and very nice with me. One day they asked me to go fishing with them in a boat, which I did, without telling my mother, which was not a good idea. When my mother looked for me, she saw the ball that the Russians had given me to play with by the water's edge, so she thought I had fallen into the water and drowned. She was very upset. Then she saw the boat come back to the dock with me in it. As every mother probably does, she was glad to see that I was ok, but then she let me have it. She was the maddest I had ever seen her at my young age. My punishment was to carry the still-wiggly fish, which were caught with harpoons, one by one into the house. I hated that. I was afraid of the still-wiggly fish, being only five years old.

After we were at their housing for about two weeks, the soldiers started to get too friendly with my mother and Sophie. They obviously wanted more than just feeding us. It was time to think of a plan and move on.

# Post-War May 1945

My mother decided to move us to Arthur's hometown of Storkow, about thirty-five miles east of Berlin. The only way to get there was to walk because the public transportation had not been restored yet, since it was damaged from the bombing. Regardless, we did not have the money for a ticket.

We walked on the back roads to stay away from complications, because many people were doing the same thing, getting away from big cities. Hitchhiking was not an option: people did not have cars, and if they had cars, there was no gas to buy. The main roads were busier with people than the country roads. To me it seemed that we were walking for weeks and there was no end in sight. We stopped at farmhouses and asked for food and milk for me, but the farmers said that they had barely enough for themselves or that the animals were sick and did not produce milk. This may or may not have been true. We lived off the fields, collecting potatoes and carrots and other vegetables we could find. We even ate certain weeds that grew in the grass and that my mother knew were safe to eat. One of the weeds we ate was sour ampere, which later we cooked when we had a kitchen. It was similar to spinach, which I liked.

My mother pointed to the doll that I carried, the only thing that I possessed. In the rain, the doll's face color was starting to run down on my coat. She said I had to put it down because it was dirtying my coat. I put the doll down into the running stream of rainwater by the roadside and saw it being washed away, and soon I did not see it anymore. Even today, I am sad about that and still do not understand, considering everything we had been through, why my mother ask me to give up my doll. If I had been the mother, I would not have cared whether the coat was getting dirty. To me, it seemed that the clothes we saw on other people were not clean and they were torn.

All the people around us were making due with the few things they had, and believe me; everybody had very little, just like us. People carried their belongings on their backs, or if they were lucky, they had baby carriages or barrels in which they pushed whatever they could save from what was left after the war. I still see the columns of people walking, and many did not know what their destination was; they just walked away from those destroyed cities and from the Allies. (To the Allies the Germans were still the enemy, and fear was in everybody's eyes). Also at night there was a lot of looting, and people were stealing from one another. Most often food was stolen. People were hungry and looked for food in any fashion that it could be obtained; stealing just seemed the most logical approach.

After about three days of walking, we arrived at Arthur's home, which was ruled by his old, cranky mother. It was a wooden shack with almost no running water, only in the kitchen, where there was a sink that sometimes produced cold water. There was an outhouse, what you would call a plumb toilet. We would carry water in buckets from a water pump into the house from the sandy courtyard and wash ourselves with a dirty cloth and homemade soap. The whole house seemed dark, and I was very uncomfortable—I was actually scared. That old woman, Arthur's mother, looked like a witch from a fairy tale. There were also twin boys from a marriage that was not yet resolved.

My mother and I were waiting for Arthur Glyz to come home from the front, and he finally did. He immediately started the divorce proceedings from his first wife while he, my mother, and I moved to a place called Beeskow, just a few miles away, where we lived for the next four years. We occupied the second floor in an apartment building, where Arthur's sisters lived with their grown daughters on the first floor.

Arthur's mother, a toothless, bitter old woman who rarely spoke unless she had something to complain about, moved in with us and the twins. The twin boys were three years older than I was. Just as I was trying to get used to my new stepfather-to-be, I also had to accept the boys. I barely had my mother to myself when these people exploded into my life. I had to share my mother with four strangers.

The building we lived in was right by some train tracks, and across from us was a train station, which had a restaurant on its property. My mother and Arthur started working in the restaurant, and they invested themselves in the restaurant as if it were their own. This was good, because it assured us of having food, which otherwise we would not have, and it gave us some financial income as well.

The village we lived in, even though it was not official yet, was in East Germany. The Russians now occupied and ruled all of East Germany, starting right after the war, before 1948's official division of Germany into East and West. This lasted until 1989, when the Berlin Wall was taken down and Germany again was one whole country with one German government.

–

THE ALLIES WERE MAKING plans in 1948 to split Germany into four sectors, one for each Allied country: the French, the English, the

Americans, and of course the Russians. Germany was truly sectioned off. The German government did not exist, and all the power was in the Allies' hands. We happened to be living in the sector that was occupied by the Russians; Communism had arrived in East Germany. We were under the rule and law of the Russians and their Communistic ideology, and we were the most restricted compared to the other Allied sectors. The center of the city of Berlin was mostly American territory and ruled by their laws, but the only thing one felt in the American sector was the influence of goods and all these tall, blond, white and also black Americans chewing gum. It felt safe and free when I was visiting West Berlin, compared to the Russian-occupied area.

I did not get along with the twin boys very well; first of all, they were strangers and not my brothers. The relationship between their father and me also was very shaky. The boys did get me into a lot of trouble; after all, I was only six years old and they were nine years old. Whenever any of us got into trouble, all of us were physically punished. That meant a beating with a horse whip that had seven leather strips, each of which had a knot at the end. Many times, I had trouble sitting in school on a wooden bench with broken skin on my behind. My mother watched the beatings but never interfered or stopped Arthur—the man I was supposed to call my father, but how could I? I always tried to avoid calling him my father. Instead I would find ways to address him that did not require the word *father*. I never had a father, and till today I could not call anybody father, not even a priest.

–

FOOD WAS STILL SCARCE, AND many times we had only fried potatoes or sometimes a slice of dry bread with boiled, sliced potatoes on the bread and mustard for moisture. Arthur was finding ways to trade with farmers that gave us sometimes meat to eat. One time we even had horsemeat. Arthur always said he would never eat horsemeat, but my mother was a very good cook, and she prepared a dish called *Gulasch* (boiled meat in a heavy sauce). She asked my stepfather if he knew what he was eating, and he said, "It's beef." To his surprise, my mother told him he was eating horsemeat. I don't remember what that tasted like, but willingly or knowingly I would never want to eat it again.

His reaction was very funny, and we all had a good laugh about him not believing what kind of meat he ate.

Early in 1948, he became very ill, and my mother could not run the restaurant and take care of him and three children. She quit the job at the train station and applied for a local job with proper training. She became a police detective, which meant she was on call at all times, day and night. It also meant that she was required to join the Communist Party if she wanted this well-paying job. My mother was never political, in order to have a job she became a member. I also had to join the Communist Youth Movement. I did not know what it represented, but I liked camping out, making bonfires, and singing songs. We had to wear uniforms with blue scarves around our necks, and I in my ignorance was proud of that uniform. That's how easy it is to indoctrinate a child. Give the child a uniform and sing some communist or fatherland songs that a child did not understand, and *bam*, you were a communist or you were in the Hitler Youth (that's how the Nazis did it with the young boys and girls who did not know any better). That's how easily it happened with the Hitler Youth or with any political or other kinds of organizations.

Meanwhile, my mother had to make a hard decision by sending the boys back to their birth mother and Arthur into a home for the mentally ill. He exhibited strange behavior, such as burning my school homework while saying, "You don't need this anymore." He became a danger to others as well as to himself. His bizarre behavior was related to his war injuries. Arthur needed penicillin, but that was available only to high-ranking Russian officers. As he became even more ill, he was transferred to a hospital, where he died on the twenty-second of May, 1949, one day before my ninth birthday.

Of course that year there was no birthday party for me—it was said it would be inappropriate. I do not remember much of that day, but I remember Arthur's funeral. The close family members were sitting in the first row: his sons, his ex-wife, his sisters and cousins, and my mother and I. They were all crying, and I was sitting there trying to squeeze out a tear because I thought, "You must cry"—this was my first funeral. However, no tears came. To me he was a stranger, and I remember the beatings and how I was mistreated by his family. Throughout my childhood I always felt that I was in the way, and no matter how hard I tried, I could never do anything right. It felt as if I did not belong anywhere. I realize that my attitude many times was standoffish—I was trying to protect myself from fear and hurt from people, any people, which included my mother.

–

DAYS AFTER THE FUNERAL, I was sent to a summer camp, to the Island of Hiddensee in the East Sea (Ost See). There were a lot of children on the train, and a few of them I knew. I was very upset about the fact that I was separated from my mother when I needed her the most. The activities at the summer camp kept us busy, but when bedtime came, I felt lonelier than ever. I missed my mother, and I fell asleep crying every night. I was there for four long weeks, which is a long time to be away from your only parent. Finally, we were sent home, and I was elated to see my mother at the train station.

When we got back to the apartment, my mother had the furniture moved around. For the first time in my life, I got my own room and my own bed, which was so exciting. I could hardly believe it.

My mother was busy at her job, and I had a lot of free unsupervised time. They did not use babysitters then. Kids were just left to deal with themselves. They had time enough to get into trouble, which all of us somehow did, since I did not see my mother much and we had a reasonably good relationship. When she came home, she mostly was tired and slept. In all reality we had little interaction. But it was good to know that I was the only child and she was my mother and I had her all to myself.

My mother's ongoing training for the police took place in Potsdam, which is only a few miles away from the center of West Berlin, but it was Russian territory. Berlin and the surrounding area have many castles. One in particular is this castle called Sanssouci, which was built by Kaiser Friedrich Wilhelm, and the garden is built as terraces, where he in the late 1800s planted and grew orange trees, fig trees, banana trees, and other tropical fruit trees; to me it is the most beautiful castle in northern Germany. I have been there many times, and each time I have been in awe of the castle and the grounds it was built on.

My mother was told to go to Potsdam for a training seminar. To get to Potsdam, which was in East Germany, she had to travel through West Berlin. One of her colleagues asked her to take an envelope with her and deliver it to a West Berlin address. Not thinking about anything bad or wrong, she took the envelope and delivered it to the given address. When she was let into the apartment, a man opened the envelope and told her, "You cannot return to East Germany. The envelope you gave us has a list of names of spies in it, and if you return to East Germany, they may kill you or at least put you in prison."

Of course, my mother was in shock, and when it finally hit her, she said, "What about my daughter? She is still in Beeskow, alone."

The people that took the envelope never said what the names of the spies were. They said, "The less you know, the safer it is for you." They made arrangements for my mother to have a room in an apartment, and they advised her not to walk the streets because the Russians would try to find her, in case her "friend" and colleague might have told somebody about the envelope. My mother went to a friend she had—her name was Friedel. She asked Friedel if she was willing to travel to Beeskow to pick me up and bring me to West Berlin. Friedel agreed, knowing that if something went wrong the Russians could capture and incarcerate her. My mother could not call me, in case the phones were bugged.

I was waiting for my mother to return and wondering what happened to her, since she was to be back after two days. Suddenly this strange woman stood in the door and said her name was Aunt Friedel and that she was there to take me to my mother in Berlin—she did not say West Berlin—because my mother had broken her big toe.

The train to Berlin did not leave until later that day. As a matter of fact, it was dark when we left for the station. Friedel had arrived in Beeskow on a very early train. She did not want to be seen by anybody. I was instructed by her not talk to anybody and that we were not taking anything with us, just the clothes I had on. But traveling to Berlin was exciting, and I wanted to tell my friends, who lived in the same building, about my upcoming trip. I pretended to go to the outhouse, but Friedel watched me from the window, and like a good little girl I went back to the apartment and waited for the time that the train would leave.

I did not know how dangerous it was for anybody to come and get me. If any of my mother's colleagues or somebody from the Russian command had seen us we would have been dead or at least arrested. When we arrived in West Berlin, at the train station Bahnhof Zoo, my mother was standing on the platform. My first remark was, "I don't see anything wrong with your toe!"

She explained that there was nothing wrong with her toe but that we had to flee Beeskow because bad people were after her. We took the streetcar to Friedel's home. She had an apartment with an extra room. She also had a son, Lutz, and a husband. For a while, we stayed with them. My mother was seeking help by contacting agencies for financial assistance and for a more permanent place to live. What I was not aware of at the time was that the police protected us by following my mother wherever she went. We were in a very dangerous situation, which I did not understand, and my mother did not want to tell me too much, because I was too young to understand—and even more dangerous, I could talk to other people about our situation. Children sometimes say things that should not be said; that was my mother's concern, which was a correct concern.

The friend and colleague that had given my mother the envelope kept working at the police department in East Germany until he was found out. When the Russians did find out about the list of spies that my mother gave to undercover police agents and that she smuggled to West Berlin, my mother was declared a spy. The Russians wanted badly to catch her, put her on trial, and imprison her. Whoever was involved was asked to become a double agent; therefore, the man who had given her that special envelope now worked for the Russians and was ordered to find my mother. My mother was sentenced to twenty-five years in absentia. Since I was only nine years old, I did not know the danger we were in, which was a good thing, because I already had gone through many difficult experiences at my young age.

Aunt Friedel was not the most loving or caring person. For instance, I was not allowed to eat their food, because it was for her son, who at eleven was a radio personality—spoiled and the apple of his mother's eye. Being hungry so many times, I tried to find a way to get food. On the corner where Friedel lived was a mobile fruit stand, and the owner went from street to street to sell his produce. He always was at the same corner at 4:00 p.m., like clockwork.

One day I decided to steal an apple. I was very hungry and very much afraid of the produce man. Would he see that I was stealing, and if he did, would he tell my mother, and what would she do to me? I kept on stealing one apple every day, which often was the only food I had. My thinking and plan was that I would keep stealing an apple a day until I was caught. I knew that at some time, I would be caught and be in a lot of trouble. Like all good things, this had to come to an end as well. One day the produce man saw me stealing and started running after me, but he soon gave up, and I went to a hiding place and ate my last stolen apple.

I was left by myself most of the time and again felt left behind and that nobody cared. That was a feeling that went through all my childhood. I wanted so much to be loved and held and stroked and kissed and told that I was a good child and I deserved to be loved, but that did not happen. My mother was told to find another place because we had to move again. I never did tell my mother how Friedel treated me—only much later when I was an adult and I was trying to make sense of many things that happened to me during early my childhood. As a child I was concerned that my mother would not believe me, because in front of my mother, Friedel was very nice.

From the time after leaving Beeskow to the time that we lived with Friedel, I had no school or any education. I should have been in the third grade.

After my mother found another place for us to live, at 9 Konstanzer Street, we again had one furnished room with a very nice family. They were Dr. and Mrs. Korbe. These people were kind and many times gave me some candy. We were assigned to a bathroom that had a toilet and a small sink with only cold running water. We were told at what time we could use the kitchen so we would not be in the way when Mrs. Korbe needed to cook, and once a week we had the opportunity to take a bath. My mother and I shared the same bathwater because it was so hard to get the coal to heat the water boiler. The water in the tank could be heated only with wood and coal. We had to provide our own coal and wood to heat the water for our bath, but we could not always get coal or wood and therefore did not always take a bath on a weekly basis. Our room had a cast-iron potbelly stove smack in the middle of the room. We were responsible for our own heat, which meant we had to buy wood to make a fire in that stove so we would feel warm, and sometimes we prepared food on it.

During those times, it was very common to barter things, since money was something most people did not have. Bartering was the way to go. People were lucky if they had anything to trade with. For instance, if we needed firewood in wintertime to heat our room, we would use potato skins. We traded those with a man that would walk around in the streets with his wooden wheelbarrow and yell out the items he was looking for and the items he would trade, firewood for potato skins. We peeled our potatoes and saved the skins. We would give him our potato skins, which he would use to feed his farm animals, and we received the so badly needed firewood. When we made a fire in the iron potbelly stove, we would also use it to cook soups, and it would also help us to be warm and cozy during the wintertime. Once in a while, the stove would come apart, and we had soot all over the room. Soot was very hard to clean from the furniture and the bed my mother and I slept in.

Twice a week we went to a soup kitchen with two pots in our hands. The soups we were given were mostly barley or bean and pea (no meat) soups. Once in a while we were given boiled rice. We also received a Red Cross package once a month. The only problem was that these were American goods that we were unacquainted with. The writing on the food wrappers was in English, which did not help us at all, because we did not know English and could not understand what each food item was. (We did not know what to do with Crisco. We tried to put it on bread, but the taste was awful). The best items in a Red Cross box were the Hershey's chocolate syrup and the milk powder.

The German government gave us some monthly money through the social service, and so did the Jewish Agency, which was established very soon after the war ended. The other big thing was that I started school again; I was back in the third grade. I had missed so much school that I was always behind. The school hours were strange. There were not enough teachers, so we had split classes. One week we went to school from 8:00 a.m. to 1:00 p.m. from Monday to Saturday, and the next week we had school from 1:30 p.m. to 5:00 p.m. from Monday through Friday. We also received one warm meal a day when we had morning classes, which was mostly rice with boiled raisins, which I hated.

Every child was required to attend religious classes, which were held once weekly for one hour. One could choose between Catholic or Protestant classes. After a few weeks of school, my mother told me that I was Jewish and I would no longer attend Christian religious classes in school. Instead I would go to the Jewish Agency, where a rabbi taught Judaism. My mother sent me to school with a letter that I had to give to the teacher, stating that I was Jewish and therefore I would no longer attend the school's mandated religious classes. After the teacher read the letter, she announced to the class, "We have a Jew in our midst." The teacher ordered me to sit in the last row of the classroom, by myself.

That day, when I went home, the children from my class followed me and started throwing rocks at me and yelling, "Jesus killer, filthy Jew," and other mean slurs. The only reason (which I did not understand at the time) that those kids were calling me names and bullying me in very mean ways was that their parents were Nazis, just like my teacher, and that is what they heard at home. But how do you explain that to a nine-year-old?

When I arrived at home, I was crying, and some of the rocks thrown at me by the children on my way home had caused head wounds. I was in a lot of pain, and my mother had to explain to me why I am Jewish. I am Jewish because my mother was Jewish. In the Jewish religion, the religion is automatically transferred from mother to child. If both parents are Jewish, there is no problem, but when the child is born to a mother that is not Jewish, but the father is Jewish, the child has to convert to Judaism if it wants to be a Jew. This religious law is explained in the Talmud, the interpretation by biblical theologians, or what we call rabbis. The best-known one is most likely Hillel's version. But there are many other interpretations by many outstanding rabbinical minds.

I was teased and ridiculed by the children and teacher throughout the school year. After I started religion class with a rabbi, I became very fascinated with the Jewish religion and also developed a feeling of pride. I was proud to be a Jew, and I told myself, "I am special," which I truly felt. I became very active in the Jewish youth group that met once a week at the Jewish Social Agency Clubhouse, and I stayed an active member until I immigrated to Israel.

My mother had her own huge problems. One of her problems was me. She said that if I were not around, life would be easier for her. Which was a true statement, only what mother says such a thing to her child? One day she sent me to the grocery store, not the kind of grocery store we know today. The store was simple and only carried the most important and minimal food items. Also, food was still on ration cards, which you had to take with you to the shop for food, like milk, bread, eggs, cheese, and some sausage. As money was very hard to come by, people would buy the absolute minimum of food. People would buy as little as one eighth of a liter of milk—that is less than eight ounces that should last at least a day, and one had to bring one's own container. We ate a lot of internal organs of animals because they were the cheapest, but there were days and even weeks without any meat at all. That is when I became a vegetarian for many years.

One day my mother asked me to go and buy two eggs and not to stop anywhere and to come right back. On the way back to the room where we lived, I stopped to watch kids play soccer, and I just had to join them, forgetting about the eggs my mother wanted. When I finally arrived home, my mother was furious because I had been gone too long and I had broken one of the eggs. She raised her hand and slapped my face so hard that when my head hit the doorframe, I fainted. Just before I hit the floor, I told her to take the other egg before it broke too. This is just one example of how my mother handled frustration and anger. This was not the first time that my mother slapped my face. She hit me quite often, for just about any reason. It always was very painful, and I was terrified of her rage. On a different occasion, she told me to be home at 5:00 p.m. (I had no watch), but I was late by about ten minutes. My punishment for being late was to go to bed immediately without dinner. The reason I was late was that a friend had given me a bag of my favorite candy, and on the way home I saw this man sitting on the ground and playing an instrument, asking for donations. I stopped to listen and decided to give him most of my candy. My mother never knew this, because she never gave me a chance to explain myself. I thought I had done a good deed.

And then the unspeakable happened. I got lice, most likely from somebody in school. Lice were not unusual, but because of the way my mother acted about that situation, I felt guilty for having contracted them. The only thing we could get was petroleum, with which my mother washed my hair, and she kept me at home. I was so embarrassed that I wanted to die because of the guilt and shame that came over me. But there was nothing I could do, and I wasn't guilty of anything (most of the time), but that was not how it was handled. It really did not matter what happened—I always felt guilty and ashamed and lonely and unloved.

The East German colleagues she had once had started to contact her and tried to establish a relationship. We did not know how they found out where we lived. They told her that they also wanted to find a way to move to West Berlin, but of course that was a lie, and my mother and the secret police knew that. We still had the protection of the West Berliner Police Department, which her ex-colleagues did not know about. She befriended one of the undercover agents, and he in particular was interested in keeping her alive and well, because my mother and he had a sexual relationship. My mother did not understand how dangerous the situation was for us. The two male ex-colleagues became very friendly toward my mother, who was to pretend that she did not know what they were after. They were ordered by the East German Communist Party and the secret police (called KAPO) to kidnap her. Those men brought my mother gifts and acted as friends would. One man was named Opitz, and the other I know as Manfred.

If sex was involved on their side, it was on the table. My mother had a huge appetite for sex. When all that came out, much later in my late teens, I started to understand what and who my mother was.

When the East Germans were trying to get close to my mother, she became friends with a woman named Waltraut. Waltraut needed help and a place to stay and food. She moved in with us, into our one room, and we were now sharing our sleeping arrangements. There was one bed that my mother and Waltraut shared, and the couch was for me to sleep on. My mother and Waltraut became real good friends. My mother told Waltraut under what circumstances and how we had come to West Berlin. Waltraut was very sympathetic and offered to help. Waltraut suggested that she would travel to Beeskow, where we used to live, and try to pick up the papers that had been left behind and the photographs that were meaningful to my mother. Waltraut believed that since nobody knew her, she could do this at nighttime, when people were sleeping, so nobody would ever see her. Unfortunately she was wrong. The building we had lived in was closely watched by the police, and I am sure the residents of the building were told by the police to watch out for strangers and report that. People who were not known to the police were questioned and had to identify themselves. When she entered the building, she went to the apartment we used to live in, which was still not occupied by other tenants. She collected the things she thought were important to my mother. When she left the building, she was stopped by the police and taken to the police headquarters for questioning.

At that moment Waltraut realized that she was never to see West Berlin again. Of course she was frightened, and not one person was on her side. She was handed over to the Russian forces, who took her to jail. She was interrogated over and over and over. The court ruled her to be a spy, and the Russians took her to some barracks not far from Berlin. She told us later how she was mistreated. She was taken to a Russian prison and spent five years there. The only thing she wanted to do was to help another human being. Of course we did not know about this till years later. But my mother knew, when Waltraut did not come back, that something must have gone terribly wrong.

They put Waltraut at first in solitary confinement, but later, when the Russians thought she was holding back information, she was put into a cell with another woman who pretended to become a friend. In reality this other woman was also incarcerated by the Russians, who most likely told her that they would reduce her sentence if she would find out more from Waltraut, in addition to what they already knew. In other words that woman was a snitch with privileges. Waltraut, who had been in an isolated cell for a long time, was hungry for conversation and was glad to have a cellmate and possibly a friend. Loneliness was her punishment, and sharing the cell with somebody was a great change. She threw all caution to the wind, and she trusted the new cellmate. This woman seemed very nice and trustworthy. Waltraut talked and gave the cellmate information that was damaging for Waltraut and my mother. After some time, when the Russians had gotten all the information they needed, they removed the woman, and Waltraut was again in an isolation cell and never saw her ex-cellmate again. She learned much later that the cellmate was a snitch. Of course no one knows whether this cellmate actually got her sentence reduced. But do I actually care? Not really. People do many things they normally would not do in different circumstances. I know that from my own life experience. There is a reason one should never say, "I would never do that," because one doesn't know what situation one could wind up in and for what reason!

Meanwhile we were told by the West Berlin police that we had to move, which we had to do often. Whenever the East German spies came close to us, we were told to move. So on average we moved every six months or so; we never stayed in one place for a year. Since we had only personal belongings to pack, it was never a big deal to move. Almost every time we had to move, I had to change schools, which sometimes was a good thing, but it did not help with my report card. I still made only average or below-average grades, which upset my mother.

My mother finally found a job working nights in a pub. Her ex-colleagues were very nice to me, giving me chocolate and asking me all kinds of questions, hoping to find things out through me. I was used like a puppet, and I did not realize that. It was easy to impress a nine- or ten-year-old little girl.

My mother was ordered by the police never to invite men to the place we lived in at that time, which was not realistic. We tried very hard to keep our address a secret. But the ex-colleagues did find us anyway and did enter into the room we had rented. The easiest way was to follow her from work. None of this made sense to me at the time; I really did not know what exactly was going on, but I sensed fear, and I did not know why until much, much later. My mother never really told me what was going on—she barely explained anything, but I sensed there was something very wrong. How do you explain to a ten-year-old child that somebody is trying to kidnap or murder your mother?

My mother often sent me to Uncle Emil, her mother's older brother, who survived the Nazi time by marrying a Catholic woman and hiding in the Catholic Church. One time, after the war, my mother went to him to ask him for money or food, he said to her, "There are so many American soldiers out there; why would a good-looking woman like you not get what she needs by giving herself to these soldiers?" That was the last time that my mother went to her uncle for help. Instead she sent me. The child streetcar fare was cheaper than an adult fare. I was nine years old, and she put me on the streetcar to travel to see her uncle. I had to make a transfer to another streetcar at one point. I was afraid to have to make this trip alone, as it was my first time using public transportation.

She did not go with me to make sure I would not miss my connecting point. But I finally reached my destination and rang the doorbell. Emil's wife Mitzie opened the door. I was let in, and all I saw was two strangers whom I had never met before. My mission was to convince my great-uncle to give me money. So I sat there and made small talk, not knowing what to say or how to turn the conversation to the question of giving me money.

Since it was after lunch, his wife went to the bedroom to take a nap. He approached me and started to fondle me. I was embarrassed and very shy and afraid. He pulled down my panties and used his tongue. When he stopped, he told me to come back, but he gave me 5.00 Deutsche Marks, which I gave to my mother, plus .10 Pfennig (.5 Cents), which I used to buy myself a candy bar. But I felt very dirty and cheap.

On the way home, in the streetcar, I was contemplating how to tell my mother what had happened. I decided not to tell, which made me feel even more ashamed. This happened repeatedly, even though I begged my mother not to send me to her uncle anymore. But my mother kept sending me to Uncle Emil, and each and every time I was sexually abused by him. I kept wondering—did my mother send me because this could otherwise have happened to her? Later on, in my fifties, I told her about the abuse. Her comment was, "So what do you want me to do about it?" Uncle Emil had died years earlier. There was no "I am so sorry that this happened to you" or any type of remorse or care from my mother. She was ice cold about all the rapes.

At first my feelings were hurt by her shrugging her shoulders and her silence, demonstrating her lack of care for me. She never cared about anything that happened to me, even things that were her fault and situations that could have been prevented if she had cared. Looking back, I think she had a heart of stone, and at one point, during one of my visits to her, she said, "If you were not my daughter and I had just met you, we would never be friends, and I would not care about you." In other words we were just connected by blood, an accidental pregnancy! How sad. I did see her cry sometimes, but very seldom. Sadly enough, I had to agree. Once and only once did I call her from the airport on my way back to Israel from Germany and say to her, "I am just calling you to tell you that I love you." Her response was, "That is something you should never say." And that was the only time I said that to my mother. I tell my son every time, at the end of a phone call, that I love him, and he tells me that he loves me. I am not sure whether my mother ever really knew what love was or how to use that phrase "I love you," because she said that "I love you" is something that was said in a sexual way with deep sexual emotions.

Also, in 1949, the doctor found out that she had cancer of the ovaries. The only treatment known at the time was surgery. The doctor removed all her female reproductive organs. There was no medication at that time, like chemotherapy, for treatment of cancer. This kind of surgery involved a hospital stay for at least six to nine weeks before a patient could be released to make sure that the cancer was not coming back.

The Jewish social services made arrangements for me and sent me to a Jewish orphanage. It was in Pankow, located in the Russian (eastern) sector, not far from West Berlin—a place for orphans or half orphans that had survived the Nazi time. It could be reached by a local speed train called the S-Bahn. The home was created for children survivors of the Holocaust. All those children had to be Jewish and orphans or half orphans, which is why I was accepted. The director of this orphanage was a survivor himself who had lost his wife and son in a concentration camp. His name was Siegfried Baruch. The orphanage was divided into two parts. The boys were housed in one part of the building, and the girls were on the opposite side. The house was very large and came with a garden and fruit trees and a huge backyard with a playground, and it also was adjacent to a place for seniors who were also survivors of the Holocaust. The orphanage had a kosher style of living, and all Sabbaths and holy days were observed. That is where I first found the connection to Judaism and to the land of Israel, and I never lost the feeling of knowing that I am different; I am a Jew. The pride of being Jewish carried me through all my life, which my mother was not crazy about. She didn't want anybody to know that we were Jewish. It almost seemed that she was still wearing the yellow Star of David that the Nazis forced us to wear. I think she never got over that embarrassment that she was forced to declare her religion by wearing the star.

I was nine years old and was in the third grade, and I had to take a foreign language while living in East Germany, which was occupied by Russians.

There was no choice; I had to learn Russian as my foreign language. This was my first contact with a foreign language. My mother had taught me some Greek, and I really don't know why, because we had no intention to move to Greece. The problem was that Russian and Greek letters are very similar, and even today I am not able to tell Greek and Russian letters apart. Having to take Russian therefore was a problem for me, and I failed miserably, as my report card showed.

In the orphanage I became friends with a girl named Marion Levy, who was three years my junior, and we remained close friends until I left Germany. Her mother and my mother also became friends, which later on was very important to me and very helpful. I stayed at this orphanage for several months, until my mother had healed and could take care of herself and me.

It was time to move again. When I was ten years old, Mr. Opitz, an ex-colleague from the East German police, contacted us again. At that time we did not have the West Berlin police to protect us anymore. When Mr. Opitz asked my mother to meet him inside the S-Bahn at the Charlottenburger Tor Station, my mother alerted the West Berlin police. They came to the appointed train station. At that time the S-Bahn station's platform was West Berlin territory, but the moment a person stepped into the S-Bahn, that person was now on East German territory. Mr. Opitz found a reason to ask my mother to meet him at the station and join him on a train trip. The West Berliner Police, who were undercover at the appointed train stop, told my mother to take me with her, which might help her not to be forced into the train. Police were undercover in the station. The idea was to get Mr. Opitz to come out of the train and step onto West Berlin soil so that he could be arrested in West Berlin. When the train drove into the station and the doors opened, we saw Mr. Opitz, and he called my mother to join him. My mother said that she could not because I was with her. The reason why my mother took me to the train station was the hope that that would prevent Mr. Opitz from luring her into the train. But somehow he was lured out of the train and onto the platform, which was under West Berlin's control. At that moment the undercover police, dressed as civilians, stepped in, handcuffed him, and arrested him for possible abduction and murder. The Russian sector wanted my mother dead because she was considered a spy. That was the end of Mr. Opitz, who was imprisoned in West Berlin.

We thought at that time that we were truly free and didn't need to worry about the Russians trying to get my mother. We moved again, into a very busy neighborhood with shops and a lot of traffic. The idea was that this way we were safer and harder to find, just in case there was another spy out there trying to find my mother. We never found out what happened to my mother's friend Waltraut till forty years later. Since we moved so much, it was difficult to get mail forwarded to us. Forty years later Waltraut and my mother were reunited, and she was finally able to tell her story. It was a terrible story because of the treatment she had had to endure from the Russians, who are known for their brutality. Even though I was a child when she was abducted, I always felt guilty for her suffering. I liked Waltraut a lot and cared for her. All she had tried to do was help a friend, my mother, who could never imagine that anything bad would happen to her. After all, it was Waltraut's idea to travel to Beeskow to retrieve paper documents and mementos. She was not forced or even asked to do that; it was her own free will. I was very happy that after all those years we could all sit down and talk about what had happened.

One day in 1951, my mother said that she had gotten a letter of approval for us to immigrate to America. We would live in Minneapolis, Minnesota. She asked me whether I wanted to go, and I said yes. I love going to places I have never been before, but my mother did not like change. In the end we did not go. Maybe if we had gone, things would have worked out differently for me, but who can look into the future? Also, maybe there was a master plan, of which I was not aware, guiding my life in order for me to become the person I am today.

My mother had a night job at a pub, as the barmaid, which meant I was alone and unsupervised at night-time. The room we rented, again, was in a large apartment; it was small and had minimal furnishing. But it had a balcony, which I could reach only by climbing over the windowsill. I did spend a lot of time on it. Of course that apartment had several other tenants, one of whom was Mr. Herrmann, who was waiting for his two teenage girls and his wife to join him from Poland. He was very friendly to me and asked my mother on several occasions if he could buy me ice cream or chocolate. My mother always agreed. Looking back, I think she agreed because she may have felt guilty that she could not afford to spoil me with sweets. One time he asked my mother whether he could take me to the Zoo, which she also agreed to as well. I don't know what my mother was thinking, letting a stranger be so kind to me. Why did she agree? Being a child of eleven years old that did not get a lot of treats like chocolate or ice cream, I was glad to be treated, to receive these treats.

I remember vividly when Mr. Herrmann took me to the Zoo. We were standing in front of the elephant enclosure with a lot of other Zoo visitors. I was standing right at the rail to the enclosure and suddenly felt something hard pressed against my back. Since I knew from my other rapes what a penis was, I knew he was pressing his hard, long penis against my back. Immediately I felt fear and hoped that nobody else was noticing his actions. Of course I was afraid and ashamed and embarrassed. All I wanted was to run away and hide somewhere, but instead, I stood there motionless.

Again, I was not able to tell my mother, even though I wanted to.

Mr. Herrmann did catch me many times in the dark hallway, when I walked to use the communal toilet, and fondled me. He knew that my mother worked nights and took advantage of that. One night he came into our room, as the doors were never locked. When he came in, he had a white doctor coat on and immediately locked the door from the inside. I was in bed in my nightgown. He took off the coat and stood in front of me naked. I had never seen a naked man before. It was a frightening sight, and I was afraid of what was going to happen to me, and that I was completely helpless I soon found out. He told me to be quiet and just let him do what he wanted to do. He took off my nightgown, and now we were both naked. I have never been naked before in front of a man. I was ashamed and tried to cover up my private areas; I had also started to develop breasts. I was eleven years old, and this man did everything sexual to me except enter into me. And that was only because my vagina was too small. His penis looked huge and ugly. I hated this man and I blamed my mother. Suddenly somebody shook the door handle and found out that the door was locked. I was told not to make a sound, which I did not, I was too terrified. The next morning I found out it was the apartment owner, who was trying to check on me. The rapist finally stopped, put his white coat back on, and tried to sneak out of the room without being heard.

I could not sleep for the rest of the night. Guilt, shame, embarrassment, and "How will I tell my mother?" went all through my head. I was confused and got up at 5:00 a.m. and walked to my mother's job at the pub, which was about five kilometers from where we lived. It was a Sunday morning, and the streets were empty. I passed a lot of ruins, which I always was afraid off, which stemmed from the postwar ruins of which I was always afraid. At times, I heard voices coming from the ruins. I finally reached my destination, and to my surprise my mother did not ask me what I was doing that early out in the streets and why I had come to pick her up from work and walk the five kilometers back with her. All the way home, I wanted to tell my mother what had happened, and I was hoping she would ask me questions. But nothing came out of my mouth, and my mother did not ask anything.

We finally arrived home. Suddenly my world exploded. The apartment owner called my mother out into the hallway. When my mother came back into our room, she ordered me to go with her to Mr. Herrmann's room with the apartment owner. My mother asked me for the first time, without talking to me in private first, "Did you have sexual relations with Mr. H?" and I said yes. Mr. H. immediately called me a liar and said that I made it up. The apartment owner had become suspicious when she tried to enter my room the night before and told my mother of her suspicion.

It is pitiful how my mother handled the situation. She took me to a police station, where a police-woman interrogated me. My mother was not in the room, but before the interview she told the police, "My daughter got herself raped," as if this were my fault. I was alone with the fear and shame. There are no words to describe my emotions of shame, guilt, and loneliness. I was very confused about the way I felt, and looking back, I am still confused and never really got over it. My mind knew who was at fault, but because of how the situation was handled, my emotions are still raw, and remembering still brings tears to my eyes. My mother's blaming me for the rape changed my relationship with her forever. This was absolutely the worst day in my life so far, and I had had many difficult days in my young life. After this incident I felt that there was nothing I could do right, and I walked around with my head down, looking at the pavement, because I thought that ev-ery person that saw my face would know what I had done.

I was forced to see a psychiatrist, who interrogated me like a police officer and provided no counseling. Psychiatry was different then; we know much more about it today. But it got even worse for me. I had to see a gynecologist, who wanted to know whether Mr. H. had penetrated me. I did not know anything about gynecology and was not aware of the chair they would use to examine me. I saw a man in a white coat enter the room, just as Mr. Herrmann had on the night he raped me. Only this one was a medical doctor. I was told to climb onto the chair and spread my legs. He did not use a sheet to cover me up, the way it is done here in America. I felt as if I were being raped all over again as he inserted those tools into my vagina. If I had been the mother, I would have prepared my child and gone into the room with her and held her hand. But my mother stayed away from all this and acted mad and upset toward me, as though it were my fault. When my mother passed away, on the day that I arrived from America, I just stood there and had nothing to say to her. I didn't cry or have any emotions of sorrow I was only thinking, "Well, Mother, this is what you always wanted, to die in your sleep," and that is exactly what happened. Our problems are still unresolved, and unfortunately it will be this way until I die.

They also gave me all kinds of psychological tests; I guess they wanted to know whether I had any emotional damage or whether at age 11 I was indeed capable of enticing a man into a sexual relationship.

That would have been total nonsense.

There were so many agencies involved that did not know or understand that my mother was not able to care for and protect me—like social services, the police, psychiatrists, medical doctors, and of course a judge. On the day of the hearing in front of a judge, my mother dressed me a little bit too adult-like, which was not a smart move. I was interrogated by the judge, and I also had to face Mr. Herrmann, who had already been arrested for rape. Mr. H. pointed it out to the judge and actually said, "Look how adult she looks. She is the one that seduced me; this was not my fault." Again, I was only eleven years old. This was the last time that I had to look at Mr. H. He was convicted and sentenced to three years in prison in 1951, at a time when Berlin still lay in ruins and had huge problems to deal with in everyday life.

So with all the bad things that had happened, finally a judge saw the truth. My sentiment was that my mother did not believe me but the judge did. What a relief! My mother was mad at me for a long time, and she had the guts to tell other people about this rape, always saying, "Look what my daughter did to me; she got herself raped." I remember that I felt my feelings changing toward my mother. Did she forget? Or was she able to push that out of her mind because pushing it out of her mind was more convenient? We never talked about it again, but there was such a tremendous change in my mother's behavior toward me that I kept suffering silently in shame for years to come.

Our relationship was destroyed. We hadn't had a good one before, but now it was worse. Deep inside me, I still just wanted my mother to love and hold me and tell me that the rape was not my fault. But that never happened. If she had done that, then she would have had to admit that she had failed as a mother, and my mother would never ever admit to any wrongdoing, no matter the circumstances. Even now, recounting this event, I feel that shame and loneliness, but I know it was not my fault, and neither were the other rapes I had to suffer through without being able to tell a trusted person about them.

What was amazing to me was that Berlin was still in ruins in 1951. Food and money were still scarce, and the political situation was getting worse, since the Russians had taken over East Germany in 1948, creating borders not just between West Berlin and East Berlin but also throughout all East Germany. They created blockades of any item to be brought through East Germany, including any type of food. That is when the American general George Marshall came up with the idea of the *Luftbrücke* (airlift). The American pilots flew from Frankfurt am Main to Berlin and dropped, literally dropped off food packages in order for the Berliners to get the minimum of food and medical supplies. The children were standing at the fence of the Tempelhofer Airport and waved toward the planes coming in. Also the American military pilots wrapped candy into hankies and threw them to the children at the fence. I witnessed that, but I never was a recipient of any of the candies. The Marshall Plan and the Red Cross fed the Berliners for quite some time.

Many people had jobs in West Berlin and had to give part of their West Berlin money to the East Berlin tax department. It was taken by the East Berlin government, and nobody actually knew where that money went. Even with that restriction, they made more money in West Berlin than they would have working in the Russian-occupied Berlin.

It was time to move again. My mother kept her night job at the pub, and I spent the nights alone. Sometimes I woke up and saw my mother and a man I did not know in my mother's bed. When my mother left the room for some reason, the men exposed themselves to me. I wondered what it was about me that made men think that they could do that to a little girl and how come my mother had no shame or conscience about bringing strange men to our one-room place. But I couldn't even say anything. My mother would not have believed me—at least, that's what I thought. Was it really me? And was all that my fault after all? Was there anything that I did to cause that behavior of these men? I know now that it was the poor supervision and behavior of my mother, not to mention how I was deprived of motherly concern for me.

Another man from my mother's past started showing up, whom I knew as Hans. Hans was an ex-coworker from Beeskow, but now, supposedly, he had escaped the Communist rule and lived in West Berlin. He spent a lot of money in the pub where my mother worked and bought her little favors, just as you would court someone. My mother never told him where we lived; she was concerned about bringing him to our place because of his connection to East Germany. One day he caught me getting off the bus after school. I was walking home, and he asked me if he could accompany me, and I told him no. So he told me a story about how he loved my mother and he wanted to surprise her by putting some expensive chocolate through the mail slot (which was a slit in the center of the entrance door to each apartment). I was still eleven years old and basically trusted people. Unfortunately I wanted to trust Hans, and I told him where we lived. As it became evident in the future, that was a mistake.

The chocolate never came, but he became very friendly with my mother and spent a night sleeping in my mother's bed while my mother worked at the pub at night. I slept on the couch. He told me that he knew about the rape and he wanted me to show him physically what exactly had happened. Of course I hesitated because I did not want to have another sexual experience. As a matter of fact, I was terrified, and I was wondering how my mother could put me in this situation and why would she tell a total stranger about the rape and why she did not think about the consequences of what could happen to me. There were a lot of *why*s but no answers and nowhere to go with my *why*s. The older I got, the more I wondered about this situation and what I would have done to protect my child. Of course this man did rape me, and more than ever, my shame was growing, and I had the same thoughts I had had before—why me? In fact I became suicidal, which was my first suicide thought and attempt. There was medication that my mother took, and I thought that I could poison myself. What had I done to deserve this kind of agony? Well, the suicide did not work. I thought of suicide many more times, but how? I was too chicken and could not follow through, in the fear that I might not succeed and would just get hurt but would not die.

When my mother came home, it was time for me to go to school. It was a long walk, longer than ever before. I wanted to talk to somebody, but I did not know who! With my head hanging down, I arrived at the school and took my seat in the last row in the classroom. I still was ridiculed and bullied by my teacher and classmates. I felt so lonely, and the only thing that gave me joy was the Jewish youth group I went to once a week; I also continued with my religious school.

Then one day my mother told me that she was going to the movies with Hans, since that was her evening off. I did not think anything about that. A lot of people went to the movies. When I woke up the next morning, my mother was not there. I went to her workplace and was told she was not there either and she never showed up. I went to school as always, thinking my mother would be home when I came back. She was not at home, and nobody had heard anything about her whereabouts. On the third day, when I still had not heard anything from my mother, I went to the Jewish social services and told them that my mother was missing. This was in February 1952; I was still only eleven years old (my birthday is in May). Years later I found out what had happened.

The police questioned me, wanting to know what I knew about the possible disappearance of my mother. The only thing I knew was that my mother had gone to the movies with a man named Hans. I didn't even know his last name. I was no help to them.

The Jewish Agency found an orphanage in a different district of Berlin, where I stayed till I turned fourteen years old. I had a good friend Marion that I knew from the Jewish youth camp and her mother Gertrud. Her mother and mine had become good friends, and she was also in shock, not knowing what could have happened to my mother. As we grew older, Marion and I became best friends, and we were almost inseparable. We also did a lot of stupid things together, things that teenagers will do just because we are curious. We were in the same group within the Jewish youth group, which we were very happy about. The Jewish youth group was the only place where I felt comfortable. Marion's mother, Gertrud, often invited me to stay with them, and I always liked that.

I had a hard time adjusting to life in the orphanage because most of those kids were abusive and cruel. They mostly came from single-parent homes where the parent was abusive, and they did not know anything else. But I did not understand that at the time. I was on the total offensive and got into a lot of trouble.

But I did have good standing with the Jewish youth group and the Jewish social services, where I felt safe.

Because the orphanage was in a different school sector, I also had to change to a different school, where nobody knew that I was Jewish. The teacher was friendly, and I became a totally different student. Instead of getting Fs, I now pulled in Bs and even As. History and writing were my favorite subjects. When I turned in my essays, I almost always got As. Some of the pupils got jealous and started to force me to a one-on-one fight against a boy. It took place in the classroom during a break. I was not keen on fighting in general, but to make a point I did fight this boy. He lost and I won. That was it; from then on I had respect from my classmates. Now suddenly I was asked by students if I would help them with the essays, which I did. When the teacher read those essays, she asked the kids that I helped whether she should give the As to them or to me. Obviously she recognized my writing style.

My report card from this school was actually a report card transferred from my previous school, and it looked as bad, as always. My new teacher apologized and said she could not understand the report card because I was a very good student in her class. I never explained why I had a bad report card to the teacher, even though I knew why. It was because the other teacher was a Nazi and hated me just because I was Jewish. The previous teacher that hated Jews made me fearful to participate in class, and I did only the minimum schoolwork required in that school. I felt worthless in all respects for many years. I never told my mother why my report card was so bad and what I had to go through with that particular teacher.

In the orphanage I lived in a dorm with three other girls in the same room. There was one girl in particular that tormented me. She was the oldest at that home and the tallest. She intimidated everyone. One day it was found out that somebody had stolen something. They eventually found out that it was the girl that intimidated everyone. I don't know how, but she was put into isolation, and I was asked to watch her and find out about the theft as much as I could. So there we were, alone in a large room, and I had no idea what to do. Nor did I know why I was chosen to be her temporary guardian. The girl I watched asked me, "What are you going to do to me?" And I said, "Nothing." So we just sat there looking at each other and waiting, wondering what was going to happen. Obviously the staff trusted me. She eventually was taken to a home for teenagers with criminal pasts. That made me feel good, because that was one more person I did not need to fear anymore.

I was still waiting to hear from my mother. My fear was that she was dead. After six months in the orphanage, I was called into the office of the director and was told that she had some news but I needed to promise not to cry. She said I had a telephone call from a woman named Gertrud Levy, the mother of my Jewish friend Marion, whom I had known since I was nine years old in the Jewish orphanage. I picked up the phone, and Aunt Gertrud said to me, "I have news from your mother, but I don't want you to get upset." She had a letter from my mother where she told us where she was, but my mother was not allowed to disclose how she had gotten to the prison she was held at or why. A lot of the writing was blacked out to prevent me from learning too much about her whereabouts and what she was doing.

As it turned out, she was incarcerated in East Berlin and had been put on trial as a spy against the Russians who occupied East Germany. The East German pigs got to her after all, even with all the protection my mother had. She was sentenced to five years of hard labor. Of course I cried, and my whole body shook. Now I had an address, and I could write her, and I started to correspond with her. I was permitted to send only one letter a month. But we still did not know what had happened to her friend, Waltraut, who was arrested by the Russian police before they got to my mother. I think that they put a lot of pressure on Waltraut to find out about my mother. They may have promised her an early release or God knows what, just so she would talk. That may have been what happened, and then they sent this guy Hans after my mother, and now we know the possible rest of the story. But the whole truth will not be known to us until we can actually talk to Waltraut.

At twelve years old, I had to change schools. The school system in Germany is so different from anywhere else I have ever seen. In fourth grade the school makes the decision about which high school you will attend. In my case I was sent to the lowest grade of high school because of my bad grades, even though they thought I was a good enough student for them to have jumped me from the seventh grade and put me straight into the eighth grade. The high schools are divided into three levels: the practical school for pupils who will be be trained as blue-collar workers and for lower-paid jobs, like secretary assistant or salesperson—practical jobs and labor jobs that did not require more than an eighth-grade education. Then there was the middle high school, or the *Teknion*, which gave you a chance to become a full-fledged secretary or even a teacher for lower-grade classes. These required ten years of schooling. Finally there was the upper-class school that took thirteen years of schooling, and you could go to a university and became a lawyer or doctor or anything in the field of science.

The orphanage I lived at kept children only up to the age of fourteen. I had to leave the orphanage and also was forced to leave the school system after I completed the eighth grade without any chance to go to another school for higher learning.

I went to the Jewish Agency for help. They gave me a place to live in the nursing training school for young women who wanted to become nurses, which was attached to the Jewish hospital where I was born. I was given a room that I shared with one other student nurse, who was from Israel. I was the youngest, only fourteen years old. The average age to start nursing training was eighteen years of age. This was not a good environment for me. These were women who smoked and drank and used me like a doll by getting me into trouble. I was introduced to smoking and drinking—after all I wanted to be liked by them, and I wanted to be accepted and fit in.

For one year I worked in the Jewish kindergarten at the Jewish social building, which is in the center of Berlin. The kids were all under six years old. Once they turned six, they started school. I was given a salary of 75.00 Deutsche Marks a month, out of which I had to pay my transportation, which was a monthly transportation card that allowed me to use any public bus or streetcar to travel to my workplace and back. While I was working, I was provided with one warm meal, the same that the children had. The other food I had to pay for of whatever was left over after I paid for my transportation. 75.00 Deutsche Marks was about twenty dollars at that time.

A woman that I was told to call Tante Mausi was the head of the Jewish social services. She was a concentration camp survivor and was feared by a lot of people who had to deal with her and needed her help. She and I became very friendly, in a cautious way, and sometimes I was allowed to stay in her apartment to spend the night. Whatever Tante (Aunt) Mausi said, I had to do. She became my legal guardian. I was always apprehensive about our relationship because I knew how mean and harsh she could be. I kept writing my mother, who was permitted to write me once a month, and I answered her once a month. The letters had no important content because they were censored by the prison. I knew a little bit, and I was grateful to get mail from her.

Tante Mausi ordered me to take a different job in the administration that handled the compensation to Jews who had suffered during the Nazi time and for the material goods they had lost because of it. Because of my low school education, I was a typist and a file girl. But the office I worked in was attached to the nursing school and the hospital. I even met the doctor who had brought me into this world. His name was Dr. Helischkowski. That was a strange meeting. Strangely enough he was a redhead, and so was I.

I continued going to the Jewish youth group, which met once a week on Thursdays. The educators in the youth group also became my friends, and I had a great crush on one of them, who was married, and his wife also worked as a youth counselor there. Their names were Freddy and Hanna Schultz. They were very kind to me, and I spent a lot of time at their apartment, which was once the same apartment that Tante Mausi occupied. Tante Mausi had received a large sum of money from the German government as restitution for her suffering in the concentration camp. Her husband was murdered in the gas chamber, and she had had valuable possessions taken by the Nazis. She was able to buy and move to a very nice apartment closer to her workplace.

When I was about twelve years old and became more familiar with Israel and the Jewish religion, I decided that one day I would immigrate to Israel and become a *Chaluznik*, working as a pioneer and joining the military. Of course I knew I had to wait till I was twenty-one years old. At that age the German government called one an adult, and one could make one's own decisions. But that was a long time away. I devoured everything Jewish and learned as much as I could about my religion and Israel. In the '50s many ex-Germans who had immigrated to Israel early enough, before the Nazis could get them and transport them to a concentration camp, returned to Germany with their children. From them I got a dose of what an Israeli was like. They were brash and rude and spoiled by their parents. The Jews that were able to leave Europe and escape from the Nazis brought their children up differently than the European children were brought up. It was 1955 and I was fifteen years old.

One night, the phone that was in the hallway of the nursing school, the only one we had, rang in the middle of the night. It kept ringing and ringing, and I finally peeled myself out of my bed and answered the phone. The watchman at the gate told me that my mother was at the gate and he was sending her up to my room. I did not believe him and told him that that was a bad joke. He said this was no joke. He asked whether I would like to talk to her, and I said yes. Then this female voice came on the phone, and I knew then that it was my mother. We had not seen each other since her abduction in February of 1952, and she was released in May of 1955. My emotions went wild—what did she look like, how would she treat me, and would I be able to love her? I know this sounds crazy, but I was not overjoyed to see her. After all we did not have a good relationship before she was kidnapped. I lived on the fourth floor, no elevator, and I saw this woman coming up the stairs in the same green coat she was wearing when she was abducted. When she was close enough to me she lifted up her face, looking up the stairs. I did not move; I just stood there not knowing what to do. Finally she reached the top floor, and she said, "I am your mother," and I said, "I know." We embraced, and I remember for a second or so she held me tight and gave me a kiss. I led her to my room, which I shared with a student nurse, and I do not recall any conversation, just that we were sitting on the edge of my bed and not knowing what to say to each other. She got undressed and climbed into my bed—it was just like old times, she and I sharing a bed again. We kind of cuddled up and finally fell asleep.

The next morning we had breakfast, which was not much because I did not have a lot of food or money. Then I told her, even though it was Saturday, that I had to travel to see Tante Mausi and try to get some money. It seemed like a long bus ride, and when I finally arrived at Tante Mausi's apartment, I told her that my mother had been released and was now in my room at the Jewish hospital nurses' school. Mausi and her boyfriend were driving around in his car running errands, and I was embarrassed that Mausi had nothing to say to me. I finally asked her for money so I could buy food and hygiene items like a toothbrush and soap and other things. She gave me 50.00 Deutsche Marks. When I returned to my room, my mother had cleaned the room (which was always a mess), and I showed her the money and suggested we go shopping for the essentials she needed. I also asked her if she wanted to go to see a movie, which I thought she had not done since she was kidnapped. She liked that, but I can't remember what movie we saw, I just know it was a comedy. I thought she needed something to laugh about. On the following Monday I went back to the Jewish Agency and asked that organization to help me to settle my mother and get her money from the social fund, which was available for poor people. We also went to the social services of the German government to get financial help. We received the money and assistance we needed. My mother kept telling me how adult-like I acted, and she seemed kind of surprised. It was time to sit down and find out what had happened to her. She told me that the man named Hans, the same one that raped me, had invited her to a movie, and when she reached the car she saw Hans, who drove the car, and a stranger sitting in the back seat behind the passenger seat. She was told to sit next to the driver. She inquired who that man was and was told it was a friend of Hans's. Not thinking about anything bad, she got into the car, and they drove off. Hans said that they needed to make a stop before the movie. They did, but they did not tell my mother why they had to make a stop. Later it became clear that this Hans had called the East German border police and let them know that they had my mother in the car and they needed free passage into the Russian sector without being stopped. All that became clear much later. After the stop they raced toward the Brandenburg Gate, which was the border to the Russian sector. My mother asked them where they were going, and at that point the man behind my mother used chloroform, which he put over her nose and mouth, and a leather string that he wrapped around my mother's throat, which caused her to become unconscious. When she came to, she was taken to a room without a bunk or bed and was told to face the wall. At that point she thought she would be shot. All of what happened reminded her of the SS and how they had treated her then. She stayed in this facility, which was just meters from West Berlin, for five months. It took weeks before they brought her before a judge, who told her that she was a spy and spies could be hanged or given hard labor for up to ten years. My mother explained that she had no clue what was in the envelope her colleagues had given her and which she had delivered in West Berlin. The hearing process took weeks, and she was not given a defense lawyer.

At one point she stopped talking to me and said that she would tell me more later when she was able to talk about it. As curious as I was, I understood how difficult it was for her to talk about her ordeal. I felt so sorry for her and told her how mad and disgusted I was that Hans had done this to her. She did not know that the same man who abducted her had raped me less than two months before he abducted her. Unfortunately it was my mother's fault that he raped me. In her stupidity, she told him that a man had raped me and was sentenced to three years in jail. Even then, my mother let Hans spend the night in her bed while she was working nights at the pub. That inhuman son of a bitch had the gall to call me to the bed, while I was sleeping on the couch, in the same room (as usual), and I had to show him what the rapist did to me and what I had to do to him. That was the straw that broke the camel's back. I started hating my mother, and even now I was not able to tell her what happened to me, because it was too shameful.

Now that she was back and had served her unfair punishment, we did not have to be careful anymore about where we lived, and we did not have to move anymore every six months the way we used to. My mother rekindled a relationship with a man called Guenther, whom I knew, and who at any opportunity had exposed himself to me (when I was ten). Why was I over and over and over put into these compromising sexual situations, again and again, how could my mother not ever see what was happening? Did I have a stamp on my forehead that read, "Please abuse and rape me?" Becoming a loving daughter was not natural to me, because I blamed my mother for my misery—something that followed our relationship all our lives. It seemed as if nothing had changed and I was on my own again. People called me rude, hardheaded, and aggressive. But on the other hand, I was funny and had a good sense of humor, which, I am convinced today, helped me to overcome a lot of heartache. Thank goodness I still have a sense of humor and I use it every day. It is a cynical one, but most people get it.

The same Tante Mausi from the Jewish Family Service, who was very nice to me during my mother's absence, now put me in an impossible, hurtful spot. She said to me, "You have to choose between your mother and me." That was a huge shock to me, and I did not see it coming. I explained to her that no matter what, my mother was my mother and it was not fair to make me choose. I begged her to remain a friend to me, which she was, a friend, except that my mother was my mother—after all I was a fully orphaned teenager for so many years, and now I had my mother back, the only real family I had and knew. I remember it as if it happened yesterday. I was standing in the doorway of her office, crying and begging, but nothing moved her, and her decision was final. I was out of her life, just like that, with no emotion from her. After that conversation, we saw each other only seldom, mostly at official Jewish functions, where she ignored me. I told my mother about the conversation, and she became bitter against Tante Mausi, who was also our social worker, and we depended on her for financial help. It became a very difficult situation, and Mausi made it more difficult for my mother and me. I was the one that was punished by Mausi's attitude, not my mother. This was one more person in my life that chose not to care about me and convinced me not to care about myself, just like so many others in my life, including my mother. For as long as I can remember, my mother blamed our bad relationship on Mausi, even though Mausi was not in my life at all.

My friends Hanna and Freddie were trying to get Mausi and me together at their apartment, in the hope that we could make up. But that did not work either, because Mausi refused to talk to me while having coffee and cake at my friends' house. Now I understood why Mausi did not have a relationship with her son and grandchildren, who lived in Holland.

Shortly after my mother and I found a furnished room in somebody else's apartment to live in, my mother went back to work at the same pub she had worked at before she was abducted. Frau Holtz, the owner of the pub, was always very nice to me and very generous. I could eat the peanuts that were put out in small bowls along the bar counter. Again, I spent a lot of mornings picking up my mother from her job, before I went to work, just to make sure she was ok.

At the pub she met a man named Bernhard, who was divorced, with no kids, and he was an alcoholic. He had a great-paying job as a wood floor master—if he was able to get to his job, because so many times he was too drunk to find the bus he needed to take to work. He was laying out the parquets in new buildings and he was really good at that. Some of his formation of the woodwork was totally amazing. Most often he left for work straight from the pub without sleeping. My mother and Bernhard liked each other, which I did not understand then, but I did understand it later in life, when I realized why they needed each other. I did not like any man my mother had affairs with; I was always afraid of them and was not very friendly with any of them. Who can blame me?

My mother had barely any clothes, so she asked me one day if I would go with her to one of the Jewish shops that sold women's clothing. My mother wanted to see if I could talk the owner into letting her buy a dress, and she would pay it off later. I knew the owner of the shop, who had a daughter that I saw often at the Jewish youth group. He did let my mother choose a dress without immediate payment. This was my mother's first "shopping spree" since her release from jail. My mother never paid for the dress, and I was embarrassed, because I knew the shop owner's daughter as a friend. My mother also asked me to go to a lady I was working with at the Jewish Community Center and ask to borrow money so she could buy meat and prepare a meal for us. "Us" included Bernhard, whom I was always in defiance against. Only a few of my friends understood me, even though I did not talk about the rapes or sexual abuse, which was too embarrassing. Many times Bernhard slept in the bed, the bed my mother and I shared. Even though Bernhard was drunk most of the time, he never touched me. But what kind of an arrangement was this, that a strange man slept in the same bed with a teenager, the daughter of the woman he dated? We were three people in that bed, my mother, Bernhard and I. Why, why did my mother allow him to sleep in our bed many times without her being there?

My mother and I had a lot of loud and mean arguments, and we fought a lot. I could tell that I was in her way. When she could not handle me anymore, she called the Berliner social services and told them that I was unruly and that I needed to be taken to a home for difficult teenagers. That happened in the same year after she returned (1955). I was picked up by a social worker (who almost put me in handcuffs) and taken to a home for difficult teens; it was an all-girls boarding home as well as an orphanage. You either had to go to school or had to work. That was a condition of living in this home.

The home gave us furlough, and we were permitted to leave the building, but we had to be home by 9:00 p.m. I kept going to the Jewish Community Center every Thursday. I was now old enough to advance to an older and more mature group in the Jewish Youth Center. And it continued to be my favorite place to go.

I also spent a lot of time with my friends Freddie and Hanna, who were both born in Berlin. Their parents immigrated to Israel in the late 1930s. They remained in Israel while their children returned to Berlin in the early '50s. They were the group leaders and counselors for the children at the Jewish Community Center, where children came to sing, read, play games, and organize crafts, and they also created a theater group. Once a year we were taken to summer camp in the Black Forest in Germany, which was sponsored by a Jewish agency. It was a beautiful spot because you could see the German Alps with the highest peak of the Watzmann, which was always covered with snow. We had that view from the building we occupied. It also had a lot of walking areas through the forest. It was my favorite time of the year. I became like a trusted person at the orphanage and made friends with the youngsters and the staff.

While I lived in Berlin, I saw my mother very seldom. The night before I turned seventeen, my mother called me at work and asked me to come and spend a night in her rented room. I did go and spend the night, sleeping on the couch, but then it happened. My mother told me that I could celebrate my birthday with her. But my friend Hanna had already told me she would give me a birthday party, since we did not know whether my mother would be available since she spent all her time with Bernhard. It was not certain that she would be there for my birthday. Of course I was overjoyed that somebody would throw me a birthday party, and I was looking forward to the party.

When I arrived at my mother's place to spend the night, she told me about the party that she had planned for me, and I told her that my friends had already made arrangements and that I accepted. So on the eve of my birthday, my mother said, "If you go to your friend's for your party, then you might as well pack your things, and don't bother to ever come back. I am done with you. You have until tomorrow morning to make up your mind." Sleep was almost impossible. I tossed and turned and told my mother it was not fair that she showed up one day before my birthday with such an ultimatum. Who does that?

The next morning my mother asked me again if I would come back for the party after work, and I said, "No. My friends have had this planned for days, and I will not let them down."

My mother ordered me to pack my things in one very old suitcase and leave and not to come back. So I went to work with a suitcase in my hand, and that is how I showed up at work. My colleagues asked me what that meant, and I told them that my mother had thrown me out of the house and I would spend the night with my friends before I went back to the orphanage. Some-body made me a present and gave me flowers, and I even got cake. At 5:00 p.m. I left work and went to my friend's house with my suitcase in my hand. It was a bittersweet seventeenth-year birthday, but I was with people who cared about me, and I loved these people. They had cake, candles, flowers, and presents. For a while I forgot my mother and our situation.

The next day life went back to normal. I returned to the orphanage, and I went to work as usual. A few days later, I was told to leave, and that my mother was now my official guardian and I had to live with her. I packed up my belongings, which were not much, and went to the rented room my mother had. It had a couch and a bed and some other essential furniture.

At least I did not have to share my sleeping area. But the fact is that my mother was very rarely there because she lived with her boyfriend, Bernhard. Once in a while I visited her there, but I did not like it.

In one of my fights with my mother, she told me that when she found out that she was pregnant with me, she contacted a lady who did abortions. And she went on to tell me that after she made the appointment for an abortion, she got to the door of the abortionist and got scared. She was afraid to die during the abortion or because of the abortion. She turned around and went home to tell her mother that she was pregnant by Yanis Liniratos, the Greek man from the Greek embassy. So somehow it is a miracle that I am in this world. But what mother tells her child that the child was not wanted? To top it off, she said, "I do not like children, and I never did." Somehow that fact was very clear to me, as I was never praised and was never told that I was loved by her.

Soon after I left the young adults' home, I found a job with the Berlin government, punching IBM Hollerith cards. The cards had the names and dates of the deaths of all soldiers that died during the war. This job gave me a steady income, and it gave me a chance to live on my own. I found a furnished room just for me, which made me feel so good—it seemed that I was finally an adult. The room was very close to the apartment of my friends Hanna and Freddie and the Jewish Youth Club. My mother never questioned my decision to move out; besides, she did not live with me anyway. But I just wanted to be on my own and to create my future without drama and arguments.

I must say one thing about my mother's behavior. At age twenty she had lost the man that was to marry her, who was deported back to Greece by the Nazis. They deported everybody who was a foreigner. Her mother was in a hospital and my mother was pregnant, unknowingly. Her mother died three months after my birth, when my mother was just twenty-one years old. Her whole world fell apart, and she feared to be transported to a concentration camp, after she already had been forced into a labor camp for two years, six weeks after my birth. The concentration camp, and the fear of it, was something that was always on her mind. Already she had lost some of her family to the Nazis, and she had nowhere to turn to. She had one friend, Sophie, whom she could totally trust, but that was all. It must have been a very difficult situation for a young woman who was brought up in a large, supportive, loving family. Thank goodness she eventually met Arthur, a German soldier, who helped her find a safer place for me in late 1942 outside Berlin. My mother was not prepared for the heartache that happened so suddenly and all at once. Some of her beloved family members were already picked up by the Nazis and murdered in the Buchenwald concentration camp as early as 1938, when she was only nineteen years old. She adored her mother and was afraid to lose her to the Nazis. All Jews had that problem, dealing with losing their families, and their own lives, to the death squad of the Nazis.

My mother started to hate being Jewish and anything that had to do with Jews. She blamed the Jews for what had happened to her and her family. As long as I can remember, she cursed the fact that she was born Jewish. She gave me a hard time about my pro-Israel stand and my very pro-Jewish stand. I love everything Jewish, and I am proud to be a Jew. That was something she never understood. That's why she blocked my immigrating to Israel as long as I was not twenty-one years old, and even then she was totally against it and caused all kinds of problems for me. Once I was away from Germany and I looked back on our relationship, I started to understand some of her hate. Everything she loved had been taken away from her, in the blink of an eye, because of Judaism.

I told my mother that I understood the difficult times she had gone through when she was a young woman, and because of that, I could forgive her for some of the mistakes she made with me. She herself never apologized for her hate. After all I did not want her to have such a difficult time, but blaming me for what I felt was hurtful because of her slurs against me and how she was brought up by her Jewish family.

One day in 1958, when I walked into the building where my friend Hanna lived, I saw a middle-aged couple. They looked very elegant, and the man had a face that seemed kind and very humane. He had humanity written all over his face, something I had never noticed before on any person I knew. I inquired through my friend Hanna who these people were, and she told me that they were from Israel and had spent the summer in Berlin, their hometown, before the Nazi time. I was fascinated by their elegance and their friendly faces. I also asked my friends whether they knew their names, and they did: they were Anya and Hans Schragenheim.

My mother and her now-husband Bernhard bought a pub in a different section of Berlin. Once in a while, I did go there to see my mother. I still did not like Bernhard, and according to him, he heard me asking my mother, "What are you doing with that alcoholic?" Of course, that did not contribute to a better or good relationship with my mother or with Bernhard. They had rented an apartment above the pub, and they also had a dog, a German shepherd named Lars. I loved that dog, and when I was at the pub I spent a lot of time with him.

The relationship with my mother had not changed. She told Bernhard all the bad things about me (except about the rape, the one she knew of). The lies she told about me were very damaging, and Bernhard, not knowing any better, believed her, and of course that made him dislike me even more because, my mother painted such a bad picture of me. I asked my mother whether she would give me permission to immigrate to

Israel, and her answer was a defiant "no. Not as long as I have control over you."

I kept busy in the Jewish youth group and became a trustee for the younger children. That made me very proud. I helped create programs and workshops, and of course I had my job. Many times I was not able to stretch my money from paycheck to paycheck. But I had no training in how to budget my income. I made a lot of mistakes, and many times the money ran out before the next paycheck, which was handed out only once a month in cash. So I went back to showing up at dinnertimes at my friends' house. They were always welcoming to me, even though I showed up without warning or invitation from them. I kept running into the Schragenheims, who occupied the apartment above my friends. I also ran into Tante Mausi on special occasions, and she would never talk to me; it was as if she did not know me at all. I also did dumb things like going to a very expensive restaurant and ordering an expensive meal without being able to pay for it. But I was so hungry, and I hoped that if I flirted with the maître d', he would not charge me for the meal. But I also knew that I was putting myself into the position of possibly having to perform a sexual act. I knew that this was a bad decision, and I was not more than a prostitute. The man did not charge me for the meal but insisted on walking me home. I walked to the building where my friends lived, instead of to my own building. Of course he tried to have sex with me, but I told him that I lived there with my friends and he could not come in. After he tried to seduce me, I told him I had to go. I entered the building of my friends; it was very late, and the hallway was dark, and I crouched behind the main door to the building, in the hallway, till the man left. Then I left to go to my own place. I knew what I had done, and I felt cheap, but hunger is a painful thing. I promised myself to never do that again. And I kept my promise.

In 1959 I changed jobs and started working for the Wiedergutmachungs Amt (office of restitution, which was paid by the German government to the Jews that suffered because of the Nazi time), which meant I was still working for the Berlin government. We handled the requests of Jews that returned from concentration camps and had lost everything valuable that they had had to hand over to the Nazis. It was a better-paying job, and I liked working with the public. It also was not far from my mother's pub, which I still visited seldom.

In the summer of 1959, I was at the Jewish Youth Club, and I saw Mr. Schragenheim walking up the stairs. I looked at him, not being sure that he was the same man I had seen in my friends' building. He inquired about something, and I was not able to help him, but I was totally taken by his so very humane and kind face that I was eager to know him. But how? The same day, just hours later, around lunchtime, when I wanted to visit my friends, I saw him in the hallway of my friends' building. We said hi to each other. How lucky can a girl get? This situation has a Yiddish expression, *Beschared*, and it translates to "It was meant to be." Oh, was it ever! The saying "it was love at first sight" is true; at least that's what happened to me. He asked me whether I lived in that building, and I said no. Then he asked me whether I would join him for lunch. Of course, I could join him for lunch, since it came at a time when I had run out of money and could not buy food for myself. But more important, I wanted to be in this man's presence and find out about him.

Mr. Schragenheim said he needed to run an errand and asked whether I could wait in a coffee shop we passed. This was one of the most elegant and expensive bakeries in Berlin. He accompanied me and showed me to a table I should sit at. He told me to order myself a piece of cake and coffee, which I did. I sat there for a long time and was afraid he would not come back, and if he did not come back I could not pay for the cake and coffee. Thankfully he did come back. He then took me to a very expensive restaurant, where the menu was so exclusive that I did not recognize all the dishes. I ordered deer, which was a first for me, but I always was eager to try dishes I did not know the taste of. I was pleasantly surprised at how tasty the dish was. Mr. Schragenheim and I started talking, and my first question was, "Where is your wife?" He told me he was there by himself and his wife was back in Israel. He also told me that he would stay for a few weeks, which made me very happy. I wanted to know him better and for him to know me. This man was so much older than I, but I could not guess his age at all. I was nineteen years old. He was three times my senior, which I found out later. I was amazed at how kind his face was; he was elegant and sophisticated, and I did not think for a moment that he had anything ill on his mind. My friends said he was ugly, unattractive and much too old. But that is not what I saw in his face; I just saw the kindness and tolerance. I can truly say that I loved him from the first time I saw him. He seemed so trustworthy, and it felt so good to be talked to as an adult.

He asked about my plans for the future and what I was doing at that time. I told him that the moment I turned twenty-one years old I would immigrate to Israel. He liked that decision very much. He told me how they had gotten out of Berlin before 1938 to save his and his wife's lives. Their son Daniel was born in

Israel. They had left everything behind, just like most Jews who immigrated to different countries, not just to Israel. So did the Schragenheims—they went to Israel with nothing to avoid being taken to a concentration camp. We met almost every day and had a meal together. I felt spoiled and special. I spoke of my mother and the bad relationship we had and how she had treated me throughout my life. He asked if there was anything he could do for me, like maybe talk to my mother. I declined, because there was absolutely no sense in having a stranger to talk to my mother, especially a Jew from Israel. And then one day it happened: we kissed. It was such a tender, sweet kiss that I did not want it to end.

The next day he asked me whether I would spend a night with him at the Hilton Hotel, which is a five-star hotel. I have never before even entered such a facility. Of course I said yes and was very excited. I did know what being invited to spend a night with Hans at a hotel meant, but that was something I wanted. He explained to me that when a foreigner stayed in a five-star hotel, the hotel flew the flag of the country the hotel guest was coming from. When I arrived at the hotel, I saw the flag of Israel flying. What a sight! I went up to the room he had reserved. He had actually reserved two rooms with a connecting door, just in case

I was uncomfortable about spending a night with him; I could stay in the adjacent room. What a gentleman!

We ordered room service, and Hans finally opened up to me about his family situation. He had a son named Daniel who had died in one of the convoys that brought food and water to Jerusalem, because the Arabs had cut off all access to Jerusalem before Israel became a state. Even after it received statehood in 1948, the Arabs kept up the blockade. It was vital to get food supplies and much-needed drinking water to Jerusalem. The Israeli partisans, or *Chaluzim* (pioneers), organized convoys to supply the Israelis that lived in Jerusalem with much-needed food and water because Jerusalem had to remain free and had to be defended. The convoys left at nighttime, and the Arabs lined the road that led up to Jerusalem and opened fire when the convoys were trying to drive up from Tel Aviv with provisions. Every night when the convoys took off, all the drivers of those trucks with food and water were attacked with Molotov cocktails and shot at by the Arabs who were waiting in the brush and mountainous areas to kill as many Israelis as possible. The Israeli partisans did not give up. Many, too many, gave their lives, but quite a few made it to Jerusalem, and Hans's son was one of those that got shot and died. He was twenty-four years old, older then I was at that particular time when Hans and I first met. Today the remnants of the burned-out trucks, trucks bombed and burned by Molotov cocktails, still line the main road to Jerusalem as a reminder never to forget the lives taken and sacrificed and their heroic actions to feed and keep Jerusalem free. Old Jerusalem stayed divided, one part Jordan and the other part Israel, until 1967, when we freed Jerusalem and got all of Jerusalem back after the Six-Day War.

Hans also told me about his wife's affair with his best friend. This was something that was ongoing, even though she swore on their son's death that she had not had an affair. But he had evidence and friends who told him about the affair. Hans also said that he had never had a relationship outside his marriage until then; I believed him, because I know he was honest and too good a person to lie about that or tell me about that to make me feel sorry for him.

We spend a night of lovemaking, and his tenderness was so different from the rapes I had experienced. Of course it was not the most exiting night for him, but I was so enamored with him that whatever happened was good enough for me. At that time, I had not told him about the rapes. The next morning we had breakfast in our room and then checked out of the hotel. I was filled with love for this man and did not want to go to the small pitiful room that I had rented.

We did not see each other every day, but we did get together maybe once or twice a week. My favorite time was when Hans invited me to his rented apartment, and sometimes I spent the night there. I was not ashamed of my relationship with Hans, and my friends knew all about it, since they lived in the apartment below Hans's.

Sometimes Hans wanted to be alone, which I was not crazy about, because I wanted to be with him at all times. On the other hand I did not want to be in his way or for him to get impatient with me because I seemed obsessive. I was so smitten and in love, something I had never felt before. This was a new feeling, and it filled my heart and body. I yearned for his touch and kisses. After we started the affair, I never was with another man, even when Hans left to go back to Israel. My love for him was so strong that I could not stand to be touched by some other man.

Hans did not know about my deep love for him. I was afraid to say it out loud, afraid that if I told him it would scare him and he would stop seeing me. He started taking me to theater performances and operas and classical concerts and also museums. He was my mentor and lover, just like in the story of Pygmalion, only at that time I did not know the story of Pygmalion. He opened my mind and eyes to more educational things, something I had not experienced or learned about in school or from my mother. I gained a lot of knowledge and started reading the German classics and also Shakespeare, Dickinson, Hugo, Dumas, and biographies of Michelangelo and Rodin and other artists. In other words I started to become educated. The next thing Hans suggested was for me to find an evening school and go back to school and elevate my education for possible higher education and professional jobs. I only had an eighth-grade education, thanks to the German social services and orphanages that did not give me a chance to advance in my education. Hans was the first person whom I could talk to about everything. I told him about my bad relationship with my mother and the sexual abuse and the rapes. We had long and very intimate talks about our lives, and for the first time I felt I did not need to hide anything anymore.

I literally came out of hiding.

It felt so great to be able to speak of my innermost fears and shame to a person who truly wanted me to be happy and feel good about myself. That person was Hans, and I owe him a great part of my later life, when I found out how to be a better person and gained knowledge and interest to learn, learn, and learn. This was the beginning of becoming me. But it still took years of paying attention and making the right choices.

I had an opportunity, through my job with the Berliner government, to go to an evening school for one year, Monday to Friday from 5:00 p.m. to 10:00 p.m. I was eager to make that commitment because with the diploma I would have a chance to continue schooling and enter a college that specialized in education for social services. Since I had had such a bad experience with the Berliner social services, I wanted to make a difference and be the best. That was my goal.

The summer came to an end, and Hans was preparing to return to Tel Aviv. It was the saddest time for me, to realize I would not see him again for a long time. The goodbye was very painful. We promised to stay in touch and that he would rent a post office box in Tel Aviv so we could write each other. Before he left, he bought me a wristwatch and a handbag. He also went to my mother's pub, in the hope of softening her heart, without my knowledge. But my mother was just angry because she thought he had used me and bought me presents to get me into bed. But I thought my mother had used me to get money from her uncle and sent me to get it without thinking of any consequences for me.

But the opposite was true; I was the one that wanted to be with Hans. In other words, Hans did not accomplish anything with my mother because of her stubbornness and hate against me and the Jews. Yes, she hated the fact that she was Jewish. I always was trying to figure out why she was a Jew hater. The only reasonable explanation was maybe that she had lost all the family members that she loved dearly. The fear and loneliness may have been the reason for her hate. I'll never knew for sure. I am just giving her the benefit of a doubt.

But I know for a fact that my mother had many lovers. One of them was a hairdresser from whom she got her hair done for free in return for sexual favors. Perhaps Hans giving me presents was no different. The only difference was that I did love Hans and never expected anything from him. Hans did not have to bribe me with presents for sexual favors, which were not favors but true love on my part. The sexual relationship we had was something I wanted very much. His tenderness and kindness were what I loved about him.

I started the evening school Monday to Friday from 5:00 p.m. to 10:00 p.m., and during the day I worked at my job. My weakest subject was math; even today I do not understand it. To pass and get a diploma, one had to pass math and grammar and write an essay. If one failed in any of these classes, a year of schooling was wasted. I was good at essays, and other students asked

144

me if I could help them, which I did, but the professor recognized my style and pointed out to the other students that they had to come up with their own stories and their own styles.

I concentrated on school and kept Hans up to date with the things I learned and how I was doing. He was very pleased, and in his letters he started to give me a nickname. He called me Spatz, which is a tiny bird indigenous to Berlin only. These birds, as little as they are, are very aggressive but trust humans. And because of their size, they are very endearing and are protected by the city of Berlin. To Hans I was his "dearest Spatz." He kept calling me that until the end, when we broke up, which was many years later.

I finished school in the late summer of 1961, which was the year I also turned twenty-one years old. The finals scared me, in particular the written math test. We also had to take verbal tests of math, geography, grammar, and history. I was terrified to fail the math tests, both written and verbal. After the written and oral exams, we were called into the room where the professors and judges were seated. Our names were called in alphabetical order. When they came to the letter G— my last name was Glyz at that time—I felt my knees shaking, and I had the feeling that I would faint. Finally my name was called, I had to step forward, and I was told that I had passed. What a joy and relief. I wanted so badly celebrate that occasion.

I called my mother to tell her that I had passed and that I had the diploma in my hands. Not surprisingly, she was not impressed. She and Bernhard got married that year on the second of January, which she eventually told me. I now had a new stepfather who was an alcoholic and a man I did not like, which was mutual, just as with the stepfather I had before him. I immediately wrote a letter to Hans to tell him the good news about passing the finals, and his return letter showed me how proud he was of me. Every letter I received from Hans I read several times, and I kept them all. The school certificate gave me a chance to enter a college of studies for teachers or social workers. I wanted to be the best possible social worker in Berlin.

I became acquainted with a Christian group that supported Israel. They had planned a trip to Israel, giving me the opportunity, if I could come up with the money, to travel for two weeks to Israel. The plan was to work one week in a kibbutz, which is a working community that shares everything the kibbutz earns. Everything is shared, and everybody has an assigned job, mostly in agriculture. Today some kibbutzim produce electronics, but agriculture is still important, if just for their own needs. Some kibbutzim even have pig farms—yes, pig farms—not necessarily for their own consumption but for sale to people or countries that do eat pork. (Maybe some kibbutzim eat pork, but I never heard that, ever).

The second week we would be on a bus, sightseeing in the land of Israel. Of course my main excitement was that I would see Hans, but I was also eager to see Israel and see how I would live once I immigrated to Israel. We flew from Berlin to Tel Aviv on British Airways. I was terrified of flying, but I would do anything to get to Israel. We arrived at Lod Airport in the middle of the night. After we passed customs and immigration, a representative from the kibbutz where we would be working and living for the next week was there. He led us to an open truck. We climbed onto the truck, which was the same type of truck the military used. I noticed a very sweet smell in the air and could not figure out what that was. As it turned out, since it was February, the orange groves were in bloom. It was the sweetest smell in the air, and I never forgot that smell.

After a little over a two-hour ride, we arrived at the kibbutz in Hadera, bordering Jordan, an enemy to Israel. The sun was coming up as we rolled into the kibbutz, and we saw small houses, one large building, and acres and acres of fruit trees and vegetable fields. We were led to three small buildings that were reserved for us to live in. Each building was extremely simple, with four metal-framed beds, which were shared by four members of our group, and a closet and that was it. The beds were not made; the mattresses were lying on the metal beds with some sheets. So we were to make up our own beds. Very unusual, but this was Israel—anything goes.

We were taken to the dining room, where we had breakfast and were told what our assignments were. I was told to work on the banana plantation, where I was shown how to trim the trees. I learned that banana trees are mostly water and cutting into the tree would ruin the tree—the tree could possibly die, because the escaping moisture from the tree would dry it out and it would be nonproductive.

I also could not wait to get a phone token so I could call Hans. Thank goodness Hans answered the phone. His wife was not at home, so we could talk and make a date. He said that he would drive up the next day and meet me at the entrance to the kibbutz. I could not wait to see him. Early the next morning, at 5:00 a.m., we were awakened and told to report to the dining room, from which we would be taken by trucks to the area where we would work. At 7:00 a.m. somebody would pick us up and take us back to the dining room for breakfast. We worked about four hours a day. In the afternoon we all hopped onto a flatbed that was pulled by a tractor and went sightseeing through the fields that they had planted. It was a much larger kibbutz than it seemed at first glance. After dinner the kibbutzniks (a nickname for the kibbutz members) entertained us with dance and music—we learned the hora, the Israeli folk dance. Of course I already knew the hora and was very happy to dance with the kibbutzniks.

By this point I already had fallen in love with the life in the kibbutz and Israel. I knew this would be my destiny, and my goal was to be part of Israeli life. The food was amazing, fresh and healthy. Breakfast included fresh veggies and fruit, olives, cheeses, yogurts, home-made freshly baked bread, fish, and freshly collected eggs from the henhouse. I was in heaven, so to speak, and had never seen so much food and variety in my life.

Of course my biggest joy was being able to see Hans, which I did the following afternoon. I was so excited that I walked along the dirt road from the kibbutz toward the main paved road. When I saw a white car that caused a dust cloud, I knew it was him. My heart started pounding, and I could not wait to hug and kiss him. It was a great reunion. We drove to an isolated area where we would have some privacy. We talked and held hands, and Hans suggested that instead of going with the group I had come with to sightsee, I should try to stay with the parents of my friends from Berlin, who lived in Haifa, on Mount Carmel, the highest spot of Haifa, overlooking Israel's largest harbor. He would pick me up from there. And he said that he would reserve a room in a small hotel for us that was close to the area where I stayed with my friend's family.

The two weeks passed quickly. The group I had come with spent the last night in Tel Aviv, and so did Hans and I, only we stayed in a different hotel. Hans finally admitted that he loved me. He said, "It was not my plan to fall in love with you, but I cannot help myself but to have fallen in love with you." Those were the sweetest words I had ever heard. Now I loved him even more, if that was possible. I was in heaven and did not want to let go of him. Our lovemaking was the most tender, sweetest physical lovemaking I ever experienced. But as they say, the best things have to come to an end, which it did, along with my painful heart, when Hans left.

After I returned from Israel, it was clear to me that I would not become a social worker in Germany because now that I was twenty-one years old and I was an adult, I did not need my mother's permission anymore and could finally do as I pleased. I decided to start my quest for immigration to Israel. There were a lot of paperwork and agencies I had to go through. The most important one was the Sochnut Aliyah (emigration agency). Since I did not have the money I needed for the trip, the Sochnut had to fund my trip, which was money that later I had to pay back.

At this time I was still working for the city of Berlin. It was summer, and Hans returned to Berlin, this time with his wife, Anya. That was a very unpleasant situation for Hans and me, since Hans was not available to me. If we met sometimes, it was, of course, in secret. I was just happy to be able to see him and talk to him and hold hands. He had rented the same apartment as in the years before for himself and his wife. Since I did not have a phone, I could reach him sometimes only by calling him from a public phone that was across from where he lived. I had to call him when I hoped his wife was not answering the phone. When she answered the phone, I would hang up and wait a few minutes to call again, hoping that Hans would pick up the phone the next time it rang.

This worked sometimes!

I was busy with my immigration to Israel. I needed to get some money together for my trip to Israel. (The agency did not pay for everything; it paid only for the boat passage from Marseille to Haifa.) I needed train money and pocket money to pay for food and lodging. I did not ask for financial help from Hans ever. My relationship with Hans was about love. This was something I had to do for myself and by myself.

I went to the Jewish Family Service to speak to Tante Mausi, the woman who once was my guardian while my mother was incarcerated. I asked her for financial help, but she declined. She told me that she wanted nothing to do with me and not to expect any assistance from her. Since she was the top person in the agency, there was nowhere else to go. The immigration agency suggested that I go to people that had survived the concentration camps and received restitution money from the state of Germany for their suffering and ask them for help. I went to a few elderly people who had survived the Nazi time. Thanks to those Jews, I was able to accumulate some money. I knew that once I arrived in Haifa, the Israeli main port, I would be taken care of.

My mother, meanwhile, was trying to block my exit from Germany by contacting the tax bureau and telling them that I owed money to strangers, which was not true. She also told me that if she had known how far I would be taking the "Judaism thing" she would have never told me that I was Jewish.

As the summer came to an end, Hans and his wife returned to Israel. Hans said to let him know when I would arrive in Israel. He would be at the Haifa port and take me to the kibbutz I would be assigned to.

In September of 1962, I boarded a train from the main station in Berlin. This journey took me through Germany, Austria, Italy, and France, to the city of Marseille. I changed trains in Rome. I was met by a person from the French Jewish Agency in Marseille, who took me to a cheap hotel. The language! Well, it was French, and mine was still only German. This was quite an adventure. I was dropped off, literally dropped off, at a very small hotel. The ship was to leave in three days, and for three days I was left alone, without any further help from the agency or instructions. Marseille is a port and a fish city, where the fishermen go out early in the morning and come back to the dock, where there was a huge fish market, to sell their catch of the day. I was stuck in the hotel room with a sink that had only cold water. The toilet was down the hall and was shared with the rest of guests on that floor. Breakfast was a very strong cup of coffee, for which sugar was not available but cream was—it's called café au lait—and one croissant.

Across the street from the hotel was an open market. I ventured out of the hotel to see what a French open market looked like up close. I saw fruits I had never seen before and did not know the names of. That was the first time I saw ripe fresh figs, which I only knew dried and sometimes got for Christmas. I bought my first fresh figs and immediately fell in love with them. I kept walking around, making sure I would not lose the sight of the hotel I was staying at, because I did not want to get lost.

Marseille is an exciting and busy city, very lively and very loud. After a while I went back to the hotel and was trying to communicate with the receptionist. When a man walked up and asked me if he could help. I said in German that that German was the only language I spoke and nobody understood me. He answered in German, which was a lovely surprise. I could not believe my ears: he offered to help me. The first thing he wanted to know was what I was doing in Marseille, and I told him the story of my immigrating to Israel. When he said he was from Israel and also was going back to Israel but at a later date, I was floored. How lucky could I get? I had a translator, a guide and a gentleman. At first I was cautious, but I soon realized he was a gentleman. He took me to eat lunch in one of the typical French lunch places, a large room with long tables and long benches and a menu that was written with chalk on a blackboard, which hung on the wall, and I believed it was the actual kitchen. I started eating food I had never heard of before—like shrimp, lobster, mussels, and very ugly-looking fish whose names I could not pronounce—and immediately loved it. He also took me to the strangest nightclub, something I had never done before. He took me to a transvestite bar, typical for Marseille. I had been to gay bars in Berlin but never seen the extent to which the French put a gay show on. It was funny and amazing.

On the day of my departure, he took me to the ship that was docked in the harbor. We said goodbye, and he promised to visit me at the Kibbutz. The ship was the SS *Shalom*, which used to be the SS *Hamburg* and was bought from Germany by the Israeli Port Authority. My cabin had four cots that were stacked two on each side of the cabin. I was on the immigration deck, which was the lowest deck. This deck housed mostly Jews from Morocco, who were persecuted in their homeland. I was the only Western immigrant. The upper deck housed regular tourists who were on the ship to tour the Mediterranean, and many were on their way back to Israel where they lived.

This was my first experience of traveling by ship. It was exciting, and I did not know the rules or how to get about getting my meals. It seemed that nobody spoke my language. When the bell rang at mealtime, I just went to the dining room. At the door to the dining room was a maître d', who checked the names of the passengers on a list, but he could not find my name. Then they checked the immigration list, and voilà, there I was. They said that I had to eat at the earlier dinner at 5:00 p.m. with the other immigrants. Thank goodness there was a man, who turned out to be the bandleader, who suggested letting me eat with the tourist diners since I did not look like one of the Moroccan immigrants, who looked like Arabs in their black tunics. After a short debate, they decided to treat me as a tourist and let me eat with the tourist diners at a later hour.

The bandleader, whose name was Dan, spoke German, and he was my "go-to guy" for the rest of my trip. He told me that he was married and lived in Haifa. He was truly kind and helped me to navigate myself through all the happenings on the ship. I started having fun and found some people who spoke German, and I made friends. I played all the board games, but Ping-Pong was my favorite. A lot of people wanted to play against me because I was a good player.

The evenings were filled with music and dancing, something that I also did well. I had trained in Berlin for professional dancing, and my most favored dances were the tango, the foxtrot, and Latin dances. Men wanted to dance with me, and I did dance a lot. I was surrounded by Hebrew-speaking passengers and wanted so much to talk to them, but besides "Shalom," I did not know any Hebrew.

Our first port was Naples, Italy. The bandleader, Dan, invited me to disembark with him and took me to a fantastic restaurant at the water's edge of the Mediterranean, from where I could see Capri, which is illuminated at night and is a beautiful sight. The tables had white tablecloths and candles on them, and they had strolling violinists playing Italian songs. While Naples was a fisher city during the day, where the fishermen sold their catch of the day and the whole city smelled of fish, which I found out at a later trip, every day the city was hosed down with water, and in the evening when the restaurants opened, there was no fish smell.

The restaurant he chose at the water's edge was very romantic. I did tell Dan, before we disembarked, that I had no money and could not pay for anything. Which was fine with him—it was his invitation and his treat. After dinner he hailed a horse carriage, and we went sightseeing in Naples at night. My companion started singing "Santa Lucia." Everything was so beautiful, and I remember that I said to Dan, "This is all so romantic, and what a shame that I am not in love with you." I was concerned that he would make a pass at me, and when we returned to the ship, promptly he invited me to his cabin. I told him that there was no way that anything romantic was going to happen. After some trying on his side, he respected me enough to let it go and accepted the fact that we could only be friends for the rest of the cruise. After all he was married, and I stayed true to Hans. I was not interested in any other man, married or single.

We stopped at several Greek islands, including Crete, which is the island my father was killed on by the Germans in 1941 when they occupied Greece. It was a strange feeling to be there and think of a father I never met and had no idea what the man looked like, because my mother did not even have a picture of him. He was very sympathetic and said that he would protect me while I was on board the SS *Shalom*.

While the ship was approaching the island of Crete, I noticed that the dining room at dinnertime was almost empty, and I wondered why the passengers did not come to dinner. I was told that they were seasick in their cabins. Pills, dry bread, and apples were handed out to those passengers. I had no problem with seasickness and enjoyed my meals. Years later when I did more cruising in the Mediterranean, I learned that the water around the Island of Crete has strong undercurrents and that even experienced passengers get sick when ships approach the island. It did not bother me. I went on eating all the meals and participating in the ship's activity, having fun.

There was one unpleasant situation during a talent show that was provided by the passengers. I had a comedy routine that I had performed many times at the Jewish youth center on special occasions. It was mostly a mime routine except for one section of my show. When I did my "Lice Circus Routine," I spoke in German, and suddenly an Israeli woman jumped up and told me in a screaming voice to shut up, that she was *not* on an Israeli ship to hear German spoken as a performance or any other way. It was most unpleasant, and the bandleader had to jump in to calm that woman down, explaining that I was a new immigrant to Israel and that was the only language I spoke. The woman left the theater in protest, and I was allowed to continue my routine. That only proved how many Israelis still had adverse feelings toward the German language and Germany. This would not be the only time that I was asked to shut up or speak in a different language, which of course was impossible at the beginning of my life in Israel. Until I lived in a kibbutz-ulpan to learn Hebrew, I only knew German. A kibbutz-ulpan is a kibbutz where you work four hours a day at any job that was assigned to you anywhere in the kibbutz, and four hours a day you are taught Hebrew in return. They give you full board and lodging. People came from all over the world to do just that. Some stayed and became Israelis, as I did, and others went back home to the countries they came from.

We were approaching the Port of Haifa, where we disembarked and my excitement rose. The immigration officers and custom officers came on board and pushed all kinds of papers in front of me, which I had to sign. All documents were in Hebrew, and therefore I had no clue what I was signing. I trusted that the papers were all in my favor, like for instance the destination within Israel, which was my kibbutz, and that I had to repay the money that had paid by the immigration agency for me to make this passage, or I could not leave Israel, because I would not be issued an Israeli passport. One of those papers I had to sign had to do with me serving in the military. The problem was that it was not explained to me, and I signed "blindfolded" papers of my responsibilities (not knowing what they were), Then, once I finished my kibbutz stay, I would have to serve in the Israeli military. Years later those papers became a huge problem.

But right now, I just wanted to leave the ship so I could call myself an Israeli, and even more important, to see Hans, who was at the port to welcome me. It was a very special feeling to be able to put a footprint on Israel's soil. After all it had taken years of trying to get to this country, and I felt free and anxious. Seeing

Hans, once I left the ship, added to that excitement. And there he was, standing in the crowd and looking for me. When our eyes met, we waved to each other. But I could not run to him and embrace him because somebody that knew him could have been in the crowd; after all Israel is a small country.

Our complicated relationship did not become easier, but once we reached his car and got in, we finally were able to touch and kiss. It was the most secure feeling I could have, just arriving from another world. He drove me to my preassigned kibbutz, which was in Hadera, which is located halfway between Haifa and Tel Aviv. When we arrived at the kibbutz, I was expected, and a gentleman welcomed me. I was invited into his house, where he offered us fruit that was in a bowl on the table. I bit into a piece of fruit that looked like a pear. Once I bit into the fruit, I thought I had bitten into a bar of soap. I had never tasted anything like it before, and I did not know what to do. I had just arrived, and I could not possibly spit out what I had in my mouth, or could I? The kibbutz member saw my face and realized what had happened. He explained, "You just bit into a Guava fruit—it is something that your taste will have to acquire." I never got used to it and never ate a raw guava again, but I love to drink their nectar.

Hans and I said goodbye to each other, and the kibbutz member took me to the place where I would live for the next six months. On the way he showed me the mess hall, or dining room, and the building where the Hebrew classes were held and where the showers were, which was quite a long walk. As we walked past the cow stables and pens, on a sandy road, almost in the middle of nowhere, I saw four barracks, of which one was assigned to me. I walked into the room that had four bed frames. One of the metal frames had a rolled up military mattress and two white sheets. Under the bed I was to occupy, I saw a dead rat and a lot of dust bunnies. Not exactly what I expected as a welcome. So this was kibbutz life?

I tried to find a broom and dustpan to clean the room and get rid of the dead rat, which I threw into the brush behind the building. As I was preparing to make my bed and put my personal belongings away, my three roommates showed up. We introduced ourselves as best we could. They had already had some Hebrew lessons and came from English-speaking countries. Again, I had the difficulty of language and not being able to make myself understood. At around 5:00 p.m. they took me to the dining room, past the cow pens on that sandy road.

Tel Aviv and most of the rest of the southern part of Israel was built on desert sand. It's almost unbelievable that the Jews that immigrated to Israel were able to create this country. The north was a huge swamp and the south was pure desert. Today the young Israelis are not truly aware of their grandparents' or great-grand-parents' hard work to build this country from scratch.

I love this country, as crazy as it can be at times.

There were more than 100 kibbutz members taking a seat and starting dinner. There was so much food on the table—food I had never seen before and never in such abundance. Nobody really knew how poor I was most of my life. All the food was set up in the center of the table, and you just took what you wanted to eat, a situation I was overwhelmed with, remembering how hungry I was so many times in Berlin. It was a kosher kibbutz, as most kibbutzim were at that time, and when dinner was a nonmeat meal, we had eggs, olives, dif-ferent kinds of cheeses, yogurt, milk, coffee, tea, and of course orange juice. Also for breakfast they served an Israeli salad of freshly picked tomatoes, cucumber, a little chopped onion, parsley, fresh olive oil, and fresh lemon juice, just picked off the tree. That alone with a piece of pita was really all I needed. Pita bread and hummus were also always available, which for me was an introduction to a typical Israeli breakfast, so very tasty. I still love this kind of food. And now in America you can actually buy these Mediterranean foods in grocery stores or in special restaurants.

Kosher food is either "neutral," like fish, or "dairy" or "meaty," which means that neutral food can be eaten with a dairy or a meaty meal, like eggs, olives, fish, and many more items, even milk or cheese. At a meaty meal, you can have coffee but no cream or any dairy food. Every meal provided had a large variety of fruit and vegetables like cucumbers, tomatoes, avocados, radishes, and other veggies, all grown in the fields of the kibbutz. One could eat as much as one wanted or could. There was no need to hide food or take it to your room. Food and liquids like water, juices, coffee, tea, and fruit were available at any time for snacks. I learned that kibbutz members prepared the meals and set the tables and cleaned the dining room after each meal, for a hundred-plus members. The food was very important to me. I did not realize at that time that at one point I would be the one preparing the dining room for a meal or cleaning it up.

In a kibbutz that large, the meals were served in two seatings, an early and a late seating. In the evening, after dinner, they got together and started singing Hebrew songs (that I did not know). There was always a lot of music in the kibbutz, especially Friday night, after Shabbat service; of course the hora, the Israeli national dance, was danced as well. Often a bonfire was lit and we sat around the fire and talked and sang and danced (except me). I just watched and listened. A few of the older members spoke German, and they were a great help to me.

I was ordered to report to the dining room at 5:00 a.m. After we had some orange juice or coffee, a kibbutz member told us to hop onto a flatbed that was pulled by a tractor that took us to the area where we would be working. I was dropped off and left by myself in an orange grove that had freshly planted trees, which needed to be watered individually, one at a time. I was shown where the water hose was and started watering the young trees. Then the rest of them drove off. As far as my eye could see, I saw orange trees.

After a couple of hours, I felt the burn of the sun. I wore only a tank top, not thinking that I could get sunburned before 9:00 a.m. I started to get hungry, and I thought that somebody would come by with food and drinks. I looked all around me to see if I could see somebody, which I did not. I started yelling "Hello" over and over and over, but nobody came. So I started walking toward the area where I hoped I had come from—maybe I would run into somebody. Meanwhile the sun started to get hot, and I could feel that I would get a sunburn: my skin started to get deep red, and I felt the pain of the heat. Finally, almost after I had lost hope, thinking that I was forgotten, I saw a wooden shack, and when I entered, somebody in that building asked me where I had been. I was told that the tractor had gone back to the main dining room some time ago to serve breakfast to the early shift of workers. I asked them, "How could I know? And why did nobody look for me?" I also showed them my sunburn, and they started laughing, because in a hot country like Israel you wore long sleeves when you worked outside under the hot sun. I did not know that, but I learned a fast and painful lesson. Somebody took me back to the dining room, and I was given something to eat, and because it was getting close to lunchtime, I did not have to go back to the orange grove. And these were only the first twenty-four hours after my arrival in Israel.

It seemed that my adventure and my new life had begun, and I was curious and also afraid, because so far nothing had happened the way I imagined it. I was afraid because I was in a foreign land, whose language I did not speak and whose people I did not know. It felt as if I were a stranger in my own country, because when I set foot onto Israeli soil, according to the papers I had signed, I was told that I was one of the people—I was an Israeli.

Since nothing had happened the way I imagined, I felt very lonely and sad. But things could only get better: this was my country and kibbutz life, in the land of my ancestors. I missed Hans and hoped I could call him the next day, but that was a problem, because his wife could answer the phone, and the pay phone was in the building of the dining room, and one needed a phone coin to use the phone. Hans intended to tell his wife Anya that I was in Israel, but he also was not ready yet to tell her that we were having an affair.

I was desperate to be able to ask questions and to talk to somebody. I found the teacher who gave the Hebrew lessons for the new ulpan members. We had a short conversation, and he understood my anxiety. After lunch we went to the Hebrew classes. I could not wait for the class to begin. Hebrew is a difficult language with different symbols as letters than most of the European languages. Since I was not at the kibbutz at the beginning of the cycle that each class had, there was a lot I had to catch up on. I have a musical ear and could hear the different sounds in the language and soon started speaking in small sentences, like "What is the time?" or "I need some water, please." I learned "good night" and "good morning," which was easy because you just said "shalom" at any time of the day. But the *ulpaniks* (how we were labeled) all spoke English.

I still had to find English words to be able to communicate with my roommates as well as with the kibbutzniks. Most Israelis spoke at least three languages, so there was a lot for me to catch up on.

I did start to wear long sleeves when I worked outside. The ulpaniks were given different assignments from day to day. One day I was working in the orange groves, and another day I was planting vegetables. Luckily enough, they started to assign me to work with a German-speaking kibbutznik, who appreciated my eagerness and good workmanship. Since it got hot early in the day even though it was September, we started work at 5:00 a.m. I soon caught on that we had only a light breakfast before we set out to work in the fields, came back two hours later for a real, solid breakfast, and then went back to work for two more hours, which usually was around lunch time.

I usually took my shower after dinner. It was kind of funny that I had to walk in flip-flops on a long beach-like sandy path to the showers, passing the cow pens. After the shower, when I walked back on the same sandy path, past the cow pens, it felt as if I needed to go back for another shower once I got to my room. I thought that this was kind of funny. My sense of humor was always present; I never lost that. This helped me a lot, especially in stressful situations like this one.

After about ten days since my arrival at the kibbutz, I started to have severe pain on the right side of my belly. The pain was so strong that I could not stand up straight. I talked to the kibbutz member I was working for and told him about the pain and that I could not work that day. He sent me to the kibbutz nurse to find out what caused the pain. Doubling over in pain, I walked to the nurses' station and explained my symptoms. Since my appendix had been taken out when I was ten years old, it could not be the appendix. She gave me pain pills that were very strong and made me feel drowsy and sleepy, and then she sent me to the sick bay and told me to lie down and said she would check on me later. I was the only one in sick bay, and when I was lying down, I felt my stomach getting upset, and I started vomiting. The nurse came by and checked my temperature, which was very high. She could not diagnose my condition and sent for the kibbutz doctor. When he pressed on the right side of my belly, the pain became so strong that I thought I would hit the ceiling. He explained that I had an infection, only he could not tell where the infection came from. I was put on a light diet and kept taking the pain pills, which were morphine pills. The doctor told me that when I got better I would have to make up the working hours I was missing because of my illness. That did not sound right to me, because that meant I had to work eight hours a day for several days to make up for missed work time. There was no phone in the building; I desperately had to call Hans. So I walked, or rather crawled, up to the dining room where the phone was. I dialed his number, not caring who would answer the phone. But I was lucky. Hans answered the phone, and I explained my situation and that I was afraid. He promised to come to see me that day.

Hedera is only about one hour away from Tel Aviv, where Hans lived. When he finally arrived, he told me that he had already talked to the doctor. He showed up with the wife of his best friend, Helmuth, whom I had first met back in Berlin. I did not understand that— why? I realize she was there because Anya, Hans's wife, requested that so nothing physical could go on between Hans and me. Besides, I was far too sick, with a high temperature and unbelievable pain. But she was the chaperone.

My pain did not go away, and the temperature did not go down. Hans and the doctor decided that I had to go to a hospital. Tel HaShomer Hospital was the largest and best-equipped one, just outside Tel Aviv. This hospital treated all injured soldiers; till today it is the main hospital and the most advanced in medicine and technology. My pain became so severe that we had to stop by the roadside so I could stand up, which lessened the pain just a little bit. When we arrived at the hospital, I was assigned to a surgical building.

The doctor at Tel HaShomer spoke German, but he did not like me to speak German. I explained that I was an *olah chadasha* (that is the Hebrew term for new immigrants). After that, he tolerated my German. Most of the elderly German Jews that survived the Holocaust did not tolerate the German language or anything German. Even the physicians had a hard time dealing with a patient that only spoke German. Being still wet behind my ears, I did not understand that yet and felt neglected. It took me years to understand why my German was so hated. I finally understood that and only spoke German when it was work related or I was with friends.

They ran all kinds of tests on me. Two of them were to inject a contrast into the vein. One test was for the kidneys and the other for the gallbladder. As they started the procedure, my whole body started to shake, and my heartbeat was abnormally fast. The radiologist did not know what to do and said he did not understand what was happening because that had never happened before. So they gave me oxygen and massaged my heart. Finally, somebody had the "splendid" idea that this was an allergic reaction from the dye and that they would have to stop the test. Which they did, and soon my body was back to normal. If they had not stopped the procedure, I would not be here today. In other words I almost died. Ever since, I will not permit any test that contains dye or contrast.

I was sent back to the barrack were my bed was. Nobody accompanied me or used a wheelchair to get me back. Years later they found out that I had gallbladder stones, which were located in the gallbladder duct. The physician at Tel HaShomer Hospital told me that it was all in my head and I had a typical "female imagination." I stayed a few more days, and since they felt they could not do anything for me, they released me.

Years later, in 1970, they took out my gallbladder. For years I kept having this horrible pain before the surgery, and only morphine injections would release the pain. After the surgery in 1970, they handed me three stones the size of pigeons' eggs. My hope was that the doctor that had considered me hysterical was still alive so I could show him my "imagination" by giving him those three gallbladder stones. But he had died. Damn, no revenge. That was not fair.

The Sochnut, the immigration agency for new immigrants, still in 1962 had to find me a different kibbutz, one that had not yet started a new Hebrew class. The other kibbutz, where I had started when I first arrived in Israel, had advanced in Hebrew so much that there was no way I could catch up. They found a kibbutz in the Galilee, the northern part of Israel, named Sde Nechemia. (Nechemia is an Old Testament figure, so the translation for the kibbutz name is "the fields of Nechemia." It is in a valley that is surrounded in the north by the hills of Lebanon, in the northeast by Syria, where the Golan Heights are, and in the east by Jordan. In 1962 it was not exactly the most secure area to live in. The south of Israel's Negev (desert) is bordered by Egypt's Sinai.

The borders of these countries were within walking distance, too close for comfort. Israel already had fought two wars against those countries that simultaneously attacked Israel with the help of Egypt and Iraq, and each war was won by Israel. Each war Israel fought was a situation that could remind you of the David and Goliath story from the Old Testament. Israel borders four Arab countries whose population was 55 million at that time; today it is closer to 150 million Arabs. Israel at that time in the '60s had only a population of 1.5 million Jews, and today more than four million people live in Israel, but they are not all Israelis. The number includes Arabs and Christians who have made Israel their home. Israel is the cradle of religion of the Old and New Testament and the second holy site for

Muslims—the first is Mecca. Not all Israelis were at the right age to fight. They were either too old or too young. Young men and women were fighting side by side. The females served and still do serve two years, and the males serve three years in the military. When you turn eighteen years old, that's when it is mandatory to serve. Females with children are exempt.

Anya, Hans's wife, knew about me, but not about the affair Hans and I had. Hans finally told her about the affair, and we agreed to end the affair so I could move into their apartment till it was time to drive up to the kibbutz Sde Nechemia. I was staying at a small hotel in Tel Aviv, which after a while did get costly. Hans did pay for the hotel, but he was trying to save money. Anya was having an ongoing affair, even after I arrived, with her husband's so-called best friend. Hans said that he had proof and that friends confirmed Anya's affair. For me it was love only and never about money.

In Israel, as happy as I was when I was around Hans, life had its difficulties. Anya agreed to a cease-fire and let me move into their apartment with the promise to stop my affair with her husband. I loved him so much and missed the tender touches and kisses, but I kept my promise to honor the request to physically stay away from him. One day when Hans and I came back to his apartment, he found evidence that his wife had searched through my belongings and found letters that Hans and I had written to each other. His wife admitted to that after Hans asked her about it. He was extremely angry that she did not respect my privacy. There was no need for her to search through my belongings since she was told about our affair.

Hans decided that it was time to leave, and we started driving toward the kibbutz. Since we had three days to kill before I had to be at the kibbutz, we took the scenic route. Under normal circumstances the trip would have taken about six hours from Tel Aviv, but Hans decided to make this a vacation. We stopped in various places, and I learned a lot about the country. We stopped at the Lake of Galilee, or Galli Kineret, as the Israelis call it, and spent a night there, and we also spent a night in Afula, which is known for its beautiful scenery; many painters came to that town to paint because of its beauty. We arrived at the kibbutz on the third day of our trip. I dreaded the last day and held on to Hans's hand, hoping he would not leave me. But I knew that this had to happen if I wanted to live in Israel.

When we arrived at the kibbutz, we were welcomed by the ulpan director, who spoke German. He welcomed me and showed me my living quarters, which I shared with three female roommates. We were about twenty young people that joined in the ulpan experience. Obviously it was standard for housing newcomers to share the rooms with three other people. Males and females were in separate houses, and each house had communal showers and restrooms. The ulpan had several small buildings and was isolated from the kibbutz, with a building for the classrooms. The biggest building was the dining room where the members took their meals, just as in every kibbutz.

Hans and I finally had to say goodbye. He got into his car and drove away. That was a very painful moment for me. Tel Aviv was so far away, and I felt like an orphan again. The ulpan buildings were the same setting as the other ulpan where I had started my journey. My roommates slowly showed up, and we introduced ourselves. None of the ulpaniks spoke German. They all came from different countries like Holland, England, Denmark, and even the United States (California). They all spoke English except me, but the Hebrew classes had not started yet, so in that respect we were all beginners and new to Hebrew. But when I was alone, I cried a lot and missed Hans, his tenderness and kisses. Just holding his hand would have been fine. He still had the post office box, and the only thing we could do was write to each other. I knew I would not see Hans for quite some time. Tel Aviv, by Israeli standards, was far away.

Moving to Israel, as great as it seemed from Berlin, was most likely the hardest thing that I had to experience in my adulthood. Nothing was easy. The reality of a kibbutz life was much harsher than I had imagined or read in books or seen in movies (like *Exodus*, for instance). The next day my kibbutz parents, assigned to me by the kibbutz, who spoke German, took me to my assigned workplace, which was in the laundry room, where all the laundry was done for the whole kibbutz. This kibbutz was slightly larger than the one I was at before. When I entered the laundry room, I realized that everybody spoke German, though not with each other, because the official kibbutz language was Hebrew. All kibbutz members had a little house that they called their home, and it was located on the opposite side of the ulpan. In the privacy of their home, they spoke German or Dutch, depending where they came from, but I was introduced to the woman in charge of this work area in German, which made me very happy and made me believe that it was ok to speak German. I was very happy there up to the fourth day of my working there. On that morning I came into the laundry room and as usual greeted everybody with "shalom" and started to yap away in German, when the woman in charge of the laundry room spoke very harshly to me, saying, "We want you to shut up; it is intolerable for us to listen to your German; it reminds us of how the SS and Gestapo talked to us in the concentration camp. So please shut up." I was in shock! Here I am in Israel, in a German-speaking kibbutz, and I am told not to talk. That was my lowest moment since my arrival in Israel. I went to my room and cried my eyes out. My whole body shook, and I could not get control of my body or emotions. I had no clue what to do. Would I have to go back to Germany? But that was not an option; absolutely no way would I go back. I missed Hans and his advice and somebody I could talk to about this situation.

When I was introduced to the elderly couple who were now my kibbutz parents—who had been kibbutz members from the very beginning, when the kibbutz was established, and they were from Germany—I knew those were my go-to people if I had any questions or problems. They were very nice and understanding. I went to my kibbutz parents and told them what had happened. But they felt the same way—that if I left their home, I could not speak German. They also knew about the incident in the laundry room.

I asked the work coordinator to give me a different job. He did. The other thing I dreaded the most was being sent to the kitchen and dining room. Nobody spoke German in the kitchen—they were all Sabras (Jews born in Israel) and spoke only Hebrew. They started me out with peeling potatoes. I have never in my life peeled that many potatoes. Then there was the dining room that had to be cleaned twice a day. I cleared the tables and washed the floor and after each meal washed dishes. Of course I was not the only one doing this job. Several kibbutzniks were also doing the same jobs. The Sabras were the ones who told us what to do. This job was like a job you did in the mess hall of a military unit. The ulpaniks never knew what job we would be assigned from day to day.

The life was not easy—as a matter of fact, it was hard labor, but that is what the kibbutz members did. For a kibbutz to exist and prosper and grow, it has to work like a well-oiled machine and function well in service of the common good. It has to function like a government with elected members, and only the majority vote counts. There was a president, and there were officers for different positions, and they had a school for the children and childcare for the babies till they started school on the kibbutz property. This kibbutz had very educated members, but even the officers had to do regular jobs besides the offices they held, no matter what the job was. The life was not for the faint of heart or prima donnas; if you lived there, then you worked there. They had a rotation system where everybody worked different jobs assigned through the rotation. But every department had a boss, who was of course a member of the kibbutz.

After lunch we had our four hours of Hebrew classes. I still could not communicate with my English-speaking roommates. But I was more than eager to learn everything and anything that would help me to come closer to the ulpaniks and to the kibbutz community. The director of the ulpan, who spoke German, when I first got there said, "You will know English before you know Hebrew," and he was right. After six months, I spoke three languages, German, Hebrew, and English. Yippee. My English was better than my Hebrew at the end of the six months. But being able to communicate and not being considered an idiot was all that I cared about. I knew that I would keep learning other languages if given the chance. I was right: because of the profession I chose, I wound up speaking five languages. This is not uncommon in Israel, but it was helpful in my future jobs and in my travel.

The Galilee, years ago, was strictly a swamp area. The halutzim, or "pioneers" in translation, were the people who built this country and the settlements, dried out the swamps in the north, and irrigated the desert in the south, what is called the Negev. They built irrigation so they could grow plantations and fields of vegetables and fruit trees smack in the middle of the desert. Prime Minister Ben Gurion was the first one that started a kibbutz in the Negev (the Israeli desert in the south), which he named Sde Boker ("morning field"). The Galilee, where I lived, has a lot of Arab villages, which at times was very dangerous, in partic-ular when the first Jews settled in the Galilee. Many Israelis at the time of their immigration were not yet Israelis because Israel became a state only in 1948. Im-migration started in 1892, when the eastern European countries, who had many Jews living there, started to move to Palestine (under the British Mandate). Wher-ever the Jews settled, particularly in the Galilee area, there were fights and night raids by the Arabs that lived close by. The Galilee also borders Lebanon, Syria, and Jordan. The kibbutzniks never went out working the fields without a rifle, because being shot at was an al-most daily occurrence. The kibbutz was in a valley, and the Arab countries surrounding it were up on a mountainous area and therefore had a perfect position to see what was going on in the valley where many kib-butzim had made their home. The closest town was Kiryat Shmona (the eighth city), about the distance of a three-kilometer walk each way from my kibbutz.

We went there on Friday afternoons to buy things we could not get from the kibbutz, with the allowance that was given to us once a week by the kibbutz. Friday, Shabbat evening, was always special: we were served a special meal, the tables were covered with tablecloths, and Shabbat candles were on the table, and after dinner there was always some kind of entertainment. Sometimes we would go to a nearby kibbutz that invited us, and we would sing and dance Hebrew songs and the hora (the Israeli folk dance), and sometimes we had our own entertainment from our kibbutz members. It was always special and uplifting, and at those times, I forgot that I was alone and far, far away from Germany, but also too far away from Hans, whom I missed every day. I was working different jobs, wherever our foreman thought we were needed. He liked me because he said that I was the only true worker. Other ulpan members didn't make the jobs a priority because most of them had come to the kibbutz for the fun and experience, not taking the jobs seriously.

There were three rivers coming from the surrounding mountains into the Galilee, and in wintertime, the Golan Heights could have snow. When spring came there was an abundance of water rushing down the hills from the rivers Azbani and Baniaz into the Jordan River, which bordered not just our kibbutz but also our neighboring kibbutzim, while the countries bordering us were nicely secure, since they were at higher elevations.

They caused floods every year. The kibbutz protected itself as much as it could, but we still had floodwaters running through the kibbutz. And the cleanup was tedious and needed a lot of elbow grease, shoveling the sand that was left behind and cleaning every house that was affected and the dining room and also the fields, which were taken over by the sand that was left behind from the floods. The children were held underground in bunkers, which also served for protection when the kibbutz was attacked by the Syrians or Jordanians, which happened quite regularly. Lebanon at that time was a quiet border.

I started to learn English and Hebrew almost simultaneously. The English I picked up by hearing the language spoken; it was not formally taught English, just like all the other languages I picked up. After a few weeks, I was able to communicate some. During my ulpan time, I did not see Hans at all, but we kept in contact by mail (there were no computers yet).

My ulpan time finally came to an end, and after six months of working my butt off and trying to fit in, I still was not permitted to speak German. I didn't need to worry, being now able to speak some other languages.

Most of the older kibbutz members were survivors of the Nazi time and concentration camps. Nobody there was aware of my difficult time in Nazi Germany or the relationship with my mother, and it never occurred to me to tell those survivors that I was a survivor myself. After about three months of being at the kibbutz, I received a letter from my mother saying, "You proved your point; it is now time to come back home." I just shook my head and replied to her that I had made a decision to live in Israel, not just for a vacation but for good. Although I did not get any support from her in leaving for Israel and I didn't get any support from her now, I did make it somehow without her help. I never asked her for money, except once when I changed jobs, years later in Tel Aviv.

The kibbutz suggested that the ulpaniks put on a farewell show with dance and song and utilize the talent of anybody who had one. My strength was comedy. I had an act that I had developed when I was twelve years old, where I combined mimicking into in a comedy act. The biggest deal for me was that Hans was coming to see me graduate and also to see me perform. He knew my routine, which I had performed for him and a friend of his in Berlin. I was so excited and could hardly breathe. We hadn't seen each other for six months, and all I could think of was holding his hand and kissing him. But of course we could not do any of that because people knew he was married, and we could not show our feelings in public. He was given a room in the same building I lived in, just for him. I introduced him to my kibbutz parents, and of course, with Hans being there, we now spoke German because Hans's Hebrew was not very good. Many of the immigrants to Israel did not speak Hebrew well because there was a German newspaper and the people they were friends with also spoke German. This was not just for the German immigrants but also for many other immigrants from different countries. The Russians had their newspaper, the English-speaking immigrants had their paper, and of course there were a Yiddish paper and an Arabic paper. My best friend's mother, who had lived in Israel for over sixty-six years, was still not able to have a fluent conversation in Hebrew with her children or grandchildren. As a matter of fact, their children spoke German before they spoke Hebrew, because the parents spoke their birth country's language and only when the children started going to school did they finally learn Hebrew.

So here I was, looking at Hans while my kibbutz parents served refreshments, and all I could do was look at him. I was so excited that after dinner in the kibbutz dining room, where the performance was taking place, I was not able to perform. Well, I did perform, but very poorly, and I was trying to stay in the background, which was not like me at all, because I liked performing. At one time, still in Berlin, I thought I would become an actress; I became an extra in several movies produced by Arthur Brauner, a filmmaker and Holocaust survivor who created his own studio, the UFA. He was the only Jewish filmmaker at that time in Germany.

Hans retired to his room at the ulpan area, only two doors down from me. I slipped into his room after dark, and we made love, and I went back to my room that I still shared with three girls. Nobody noticed anything. The next morning I went to his room to say good morning, and when I stepped out I saw two kibbutzniks that were taking their morning walk. Not thinking about anything bad at all, I did not realize that what they saw was me stepping out of Hans's room, and they must have thought that I had spent the night with Hans once they saw me coming out of his room. Little did I know that these two people had nothing better to do than to go to my kibbutz parents and report that they saw me coming out of Hans's room, and that he most obviously was having an affair with me.

Hans and I said goodbye to each other, and he went on his way back to Tel Aviv. Only after he left was I told to see my kibbutz parents, which I did. They told me that they knew that I was having an affair with Hans. Because I was feeling guilty just by association, it never occurred to me to deny it. I just could not understand how they knew. Only much later, days later, did I realize that I was seen in the morning coming out of his room and therefore people assumed that we had spent the night together. It became a big mess, and I was shunned by the people who found out, which was about everybody in the kibbutz. Gossip was ramped up in a big place like this; everybody knew everything about everybody. Instead of explaining myself, that I had just gone to his room to wake him up, which was the truth, I said nothing. They were just guessing, and it never occurred to me just to explain the situation truly.

I could not wait to leave. I was embarrassed because they did not know the whole story but not because of my relationship with Hans.

I went back to Tel Aviv to think about what to do as far as earning money to make a living. Hans had this great idea that I should get into tourism. Doing that, I had to be trained for a job in that industry. But before that I took an intensive course in Hebrew outside

Haifa that took six weeks. It was only for advanced students that already could converse in Hebrew.

The words "Hotel Tadmor" came up. This still is a working hotel that trains people like cooks, waiters, maids, and receptionists and reservationists in different areas of the hotel business.

I decided that I wanted to be a receptionist/reservationist in a hotel. Arrangements were made for me to be able to start as soon as a new training class began.

The immigration agency Sochnut still took care of me financially. My ulpan ended in March, and a new class for hotel training also started in March. How convenient. We, the future students, were told where we could live and where rooms for rent were available. The hotel was situated in Herzliah, yards away from the Mediterranean Sea and the beach, up on a small hill. My new abode was walking distance away from Tadmor Hotel School, and I had the beach of the Mediterranean to enjoy. I shared a room in a small house with three other girls. I was the only new immigrant in this house. School hours started at 8:00 a.m. and lasted till 4:00 p.m. Our lunch was served by student waiters and cooked by student cooks free of charge. My Hebrew was good enough for me to follow the instructions, and so was my English. Part of the training was a once-a-week English lesson, thank God, because I knew how to speak pretty well but did not know how to spell or use correct grammar. So the English classes came in real handy. Our English teacher was from South Africa and had an accent I had never heard before. Different, but interesting! My roommates came from different backgrounds. One was born in Israel to a German immigrant family, another came from an Iraqi background, and another was a second-generation Israeli. We were so diverse in our upbringings and had problems with each other, but eventually it worked out just fine. We became really good friends and stayed in contact with each other for years after graduating.

Each hotel department had a schooled and trained teacher or counselor. The director of the training school was Mr. Kottler. He used to be a colonel in the Israeli military, and he sure let it be known, because he handled people like soldiers. Everything he said was an order. He was regal and in command at all times. People were afraid of him, but as a civilian and after hours of work, he was a real nice guy. My roommate Daliah had a crush on him, and toward the end of our training they had an affair for a long time, and yes, he was married. All that sounds familiar, doesn't it? I took her into my confidence and told her about my affair with Hans. When she met Hans, she said, "Why did you choose such an ugly and old-looking man?" Hans was not ugly. His face was kind and showed lines because he was older than I was, but I only saw his kindness and humanity in his face with laugh lines.

Unfortunately my roommate Daliah fell for Mr. Kottler, and it became a problem. Nobody knew about Hans and me, but Tel Aviv and Herzliah are only thirty minutes apart. I saw Hans much more often now than during my kibbutz time.

Often, when I could get away from the schooling, I would travel to Tel Aviv by bus and Hans would have made arrangements with a hotel in Tel Aviv so we would be able to make love and talk about everything that was happening within the school and with his wife. It was great to hold each other and just talk.

It always was an out-of-the-way hotel that was cheap. Hans did not have a lot of money, and that was not important to me. I couldn't have cared less if the hotel was a fleabag, and even though the hotel was not a fleabag, it was simple and overlooking the Mediterra-nean, and soon the receptionist knew me by name but courteously pretended not to know me. Many times Hans and I met in his car and just sat there, talked, and kissed and held hands.

Not exactly something to be proud of, but we were safe and in love and did not want to be discovered. When Hans realized that he was in love with me, it came as a shock to him, because that was something he did not count on or planned. But I, of course—I was in seventh heaven when he told me that he had fallen in love with me. He had thought that his maturity would protect him from falling in love with me. Falling in love with me actually happened before I entered the first kibbutz. He was holding out and trying not to tell me because he didn't want to complicate my life any further. Since he had a very tender touch and a very tender way of making love, we started creating initials for each other, like L2, meaning "more than love," or Z for *Zaertlichkeit*, tenderness. Just holding hands was sometimes all we needed. His hands were soft, and I felt the love through his hands. We did not always get together for sex, but just being with each other was as important as having sex.

However, the Tadmor Hotel, or rather Mr. Kottler, the retired colonel, and Daliah became part of a gossip mill, and soon everybody suspected that they were having a sexual affair. After all he was still married, even though he said he was divorcing his wife. All I could say was "Being there, doing it."

Mr. Kottler left the Tadmor Hotel and moved to Beer Sheva after our hotel training was finished. Beer Sheva ("seven wells") is part of the desert called Negev, south of Tel Aviv. He invited Daliah and me to come and spend a weekend at the Hotel Beer Sheva, which he was the manager of. It was a very nice weekend, and I tried not to be in their way and gave them the opportunity to spend time with each other. Still, while learning and working at the Tadmor Hotel, I was pushed to date the chef of the hotel, whose name I do not recall. I remember that he came from Romania. Our relationship was strictly platonic, and one time he asked me to come with him to visit his family, which I did. He asked me to marry him and gave me a ring. I agreed, because somehow it had become known that I was having an affair with Hans. Hans and his wife, Anya, played bridge with Mr. Kottler and his wife, and my name came up. Israel, how small are you? How easy to meet people from different areas and find out that all of you have mutual friends of mutual friends. That was why I accepted the proposal from a man I did not care about. For me, it was just for show, to steer the gossip away from Hans and me. When we visited the family of the chef, I noticed that he kissed his brother-in-law with open lips and for a long time. I was still so innocent in many ways. I knew little about homosexuality, and even after I found out about it, I couldn't comprehend it.

Just a couple of weeks after that, I was told by Mr. Kottler that the chef was gay and people were laughing behind my back. It seemed that everybody knew but me. That was one good reason to end this relationship and return the ring as soon as possible.

Instead, I received a diamond ring that Hans gave me, celebrating my graduation from Hotel Tadmor. I still have that stone, which I had reset, and I wear it in a platinum setting next to a beautiful pearl. The pearl was given to me by a couple from Lichtenstein, a sovereign country in the middle of Switzerland, and it was set in a gold ring setting. I had accomplished a lot: I now spoke three languages that I could read and write and speak, and I had a profession. For the first time in my life, I had a profession, and I actually could be somebody. That could never have happened in Germany if I had stayed there.

I accomplished all this within a year's time and on my own. I was pretty damn proud of myself, and so was Hans. Hans never gave me money, and I never asked for money. I did not want him to think that I dated him for money. But he did spoil me with presents, practical things and precious presents.

After graduating from the Tadmor Hotel, I was told that I could have a job in Jerusalem at the King David Hotel, the most prestigious hotel in Israel. I packed up my belongings, which were not much, and moved to Jerusalem and found a furnished room in an apartment that was in a building still being worked on. It was a chain of three-story buildings, and I was lucky to get a two-bedroom apartment, which I had to share with somebody else. Soon Daliah, my ex-costudent from Tadmor, asked me whether she could move in with me because she had found a position at the King Hotel, not the King David Hotel. Both hotels are still there today. Daliah and I never were a good fit for each other, but I knew how hard it was to find a job and to find someone to help with paying the rent. Well! Daliah did not pay part of the rent; I paid, and she got mad at me when I asked her to share the cost. Which I thought was only fair, but she still thought it was not up to her to pay part of the cost. I was mad at her for a long time, even while we lived together. I knew she would never change and would stay selfish. After a while our friendship soured badly, and we had to go different ways. Years later, in the 1990s, I met her in New York and met her husband. Daliah always went for good-looking young men. He was much older than she and was not attractive. Funny how things turn out sometimes. You should never cast the first stone. They also started a relationship in New York while he was still married in Israel to another woman. This was the girl who critiqued me for having an affair with an older married man. History repeated itself, but I never brought it up.

When I moved to Jerusalem, it was still divided. Jerusalem had the Mandelbaum Gate, the border between Israel and Jordan. Old Jerusalem was still Jordan. Sitting on the terrace of the King David Hotel, one could see the Old City; it seemed so near that it felt as if you could reach out and touch it. The only place we Jews could go to was Mount Zion, which was right at the Mandelbaum Gate, a building that held King David's coffin on the lower level and the Room of the Last Supper on the upper level. It was a building where Jews and Christians were able to pray, each connected by the historical Bible of the Old and New Testament.

I did not stay long in Jerusalem. I was eager to move to Tel Aviv and find a job there. I started working for the travel agency Tevel, which handled incoming tourism. When we picked up at the airport of Tel Aviv, we were hostesses and were responsible for those tourists until they left Israel. We had loaded buses of tourists from different countries visiting Israel and doing as much sightseeing as possible, trying to see Israel in an average of seven to ten days, which is really impossible. But tourists think that for traveling through Israel, since it is a small country, they only need a small number of days. How wrong they are. This travel agency I worked for created itineraries and submitted them to travel agencies around the world. The travel agencies in other countries, in return, sold the program and created groups that had the same interests when it came to travel and sightseeing. The owner of the agency I worked for was born in Germany, and just about everybody spoke German there. In the tourist industry in Israel, one had to know at least two or three languages. The employees that greeted these groups at the airport and traveled with them were called hostesses. Of course there was training involved. The ideal size for groups was twenty to twenty-five people, but in high season it would be close to thirty-plus tourists on one bus. My first job in this agency was to type itineraries, which gave me the opportunity to improve my English spelling.

That is where I met Ilse Herrmann, who was married to a man called Heiner, and they had two daughters, Nurit and Mirjam. I found, again, a furnished apartment and a roommate, close to the center of Tel Aviv, where the coffee shops and restaurants were and a walk to the beach was only fifteen minutes. The best part was that Hans lived only ten minutes away from my place by car, which he had. His wife did not know that I had moved to Tel Aviv, and we were trying very hard to keep it that way. The other good part was that we didn't have to meet in hotels anymore. I had a room to myself, and my roommate was mostly at work, and our hours were not the same, so it was easy to be with Hans and enjoy each other's company and lovemaking.

One day in the office that I worked at, a conversation came up about love and family, and I said very sadly, "Nobody loves me; I am all alone," and Ilse Herrmann, who worked there, heard that and said, "Why don't you come home with me today?" This was the best, most wonderful idea. A home with a family and a home-cooked meal. That's how our lifelong friendship started. I spent my first night at their house because the youngest daughter, Nurit, was in an agricultural school, so her room was available. The oldest, Mirjam, lived at home. Mirjam and I bonded immediately. Nurit is nine years younger and Mirjam is six years younger than I am. I woke up the next morning to whistling, which was Heiner, or as I nicknamed him, "Heinoer" (it's a German thing), Ilse's husband. I had never met a funnier or smarter person than he was in a long time. It was so refreshing. He became my idol and sort of my adopted father. When he saw me for the first time, he acted as if he had known me forever.

We had breakfast sitting at the kitchen table, and then it was off to work. Heiner had a motorbike and worked very close to where I worked. His workplace was in a bank, and when Ilse did not go to work at the same time as I did, I would hop on the motorcycle and ride in with Heiner to work. He was funny, sweet, knowledgeable, and caring, a very special mensch (a very special, righteous, humane human) who went through two concentration camps with Ilse, and then they made their way to Israel after the Holocaust and still kept a sense of humor and humanity. I adored these people, who meant more to me than my mother ever did. It's almost shameful to say that, but it is the truth.

This family became my family, the only family I ever considered family, and they took me in like a third daughter. So I started telling people that I had adopted them and they never had a chance to say no. Today only Nurit is alive, but I miss everybody. Ilse passed away in 2018 at age 102. Heiner passed first; he had lung cancer even though he never smoked in his life. He did yoga and walked several kilometers every day. We made fun of Heiner, who was color-blind, and we had a lot of laughs about him and with him about not being able to identify color. The traffic lights he knew when the light changed, but he did not know what red or yellow was. So we would say, "Heiner, it turned purple—you can go now." Or we would ask him how he liked the yellow dress, even when it was blue. Many times he would be the one to make us laugh, when he said "I like the colorful dress you're wearing" and he had no clue what color dress it actually was. Heiner played the violin. Which today, since it survived the concentration camps, is call them Violins of Hope, a violin that is played all over to honor the Jews' survival even though the owner may not have survived the concentration camp. But Heiner and his violin survived (thank goodness), and he played it as long as he was alive and was able to. Heiner's violin is displayed by the organization that calls themselves Violins of Hope. All the violins that made it through the Holocaust were professionally restored and are being played in very special concerts all over the world, including in Nashville, where I live.

Mirjam was the artist, Heiner's oldest daughter. Of course Heiner would never say that she was his favorite, but it was pretty obvious. Their common love was music and art in general. Mirjam would pick up a musical instrument, any musical instrument, and she would be able to play it just by patiently trying over and over.

Mirjam also expressed herself with drawing, and eventually she became a jeweler and made beautiful jewelry.

Mirjam attended the Beit Zallel Art School in Jerusalem. Later she went to Copenhagen to intern with the biggest jeweler in Denmark until she started to sell her jewelry and got paid. She had a unique style, and her pieces were sold at the duty-free shop at Copenhagen Airport. I have several rings she made for me.

Mirjam was my all-time best friend ever. We had a bond that only a few people have, and we talked about that, because it was unusual even for her. She also had other friends but never a friendship as close as ours. Until today I miss her and think of her so many times, especially when funny situations occur. We had more fun and laughed more than heaven should allow, as they say in Hebrew.

I also visited her several times in Copenhagen, where she worked and lived for a couple of years. One time I received a phone call where a man said that I had a collect call from Copenhagen from Mirjam, and would I accept the charges? I said, "Why? Unless she is in a hospital or lying in the road bleeding, I will not."

Then the man tried to convince me to pay for the call, and I kept declining. I heard a female voice laughing, and the voice came on the line and said, "This is Mirjam," and I said, "No you are not, you are her sister Nurit." Eventually I found out it was Mirjam because we had a secret code word that we used when we found something funny or when we did not want other people to understand why we were laughing. I found out that she was at her parents' house and nobody knew she would come, and the male voice playing operator was her neighbor, who I knew very well. It was very funny at the time, and we enjoyed retelling the story many times over. We played tricks on each other all the time.

Nurit is a very practical person. She will help anybody if she can. She is so caring and raised three children. One of them is Nir, who is autistic. He had a most beautiful bar mitzvah and played the piano very well. At Passover he read with ease a part of the Haggadah (the holiday where we celebrate the exodus from Egypt). He now is a grown man and lives in a home for autistic men. Nurit picks him up on weekends and holidays and any other times when she can. He is soft spoken and loves to be spoiled with TLC. Nurit is now a grandmother of two grandchildren from her son, Guy. Her daughter, Tamar, is one of the most beautiful women I know. When I see her, I can't take my eyes off her. Nurit also worked for airlines, after I talked her into it, and later she studied and became a tourist guide in three languages. She is the only one left of my Israeli family, and we are still close. Even if we are not able to see each other for a long time, we always pick up where we left off.

When I turned fifty, she and the rest of the Herrmann clan, which included spouses, got together and bought an airline ticket for me as my birthday present so I could come to Israel from Nashville and spend time with the family. It was my most memorable trip and the most memorable present I ever received. We, the girls, Nurit, Mirjam, and their mother Ilse, had the most fun ever. My time in Israel was equally divided so that I stayed with each one of them the same fair number of days. Each of them lived in a different part of Tel Aviv and around Tel Aviv. One evening, when they took me out for dinner, they had invited girls that I knew and was friends with and worked with when I lived in Israel. My friends were super thoughtful and the kind of friends you find only once in a lifetime.

Unfortunately the ending of this trip was very tragic.

I left Israel at 2:00 a.m. on June 19, 1990, and on that day at 11:00 a.m., while I still was in the air on El Al Airlines, Mirjam was dead. Murdered! By her second husband, because she wanted a divorce. The murder was planned and arranged to look like a robbery, and the husband even called the police to tell them that there was a robbery and his wife was killed. The police found out very fast that the caller, the husband, was actually the murderer. The jewelry seemed stolen, and the drawers were pulled out to make the scene more believable. But the jewels were found in their car. The husband was arrested, tried, and sentenced. The maximum penalty in Israel for murder is twenty-five years' imprisonment; after that time, the criminal is freed.

When I arrived home in Nashville, Nurit's husband, Yossi, called me and told me what had happened. I was devastated and cried for days. It's something I just could not believe or imagine. She was beautiful and young and had two daughters: Meri, fourteen, and Nilli, eleven years old. How unfair is the punishment for this kind of brutal crime? The only death penalty Israel hands down is for Nazis and spies.

It still hurts when I think about Mirjam's murder. She did not deserve this. Our bond was so strong and unexplainable and so very special. It's hard for me to think about it, even today.

On Ilse's ninety-ninth birthday, Nurit, her youngest daughter, had a violinist playing Heiner's violin, Ilse's favorite classical music, in the assisted living facility she lived in in Israel. I saw that program. Ilse passed away on August 18, 2018, at age 102. She definitely was more loving with me than my own mother. We in Nashville also had a special concert with the Nashville Philharmonic Orchestra and the Violins of Hope. Ahead of the concert was a dinner to honor the survivors of the Holocaust and children of the survivors. I am both: I survived the Holocaust, and so did my mother. Many non-Jews came to that concert as well. Heiner's violin was there, and a professional violinist played it. The money from the sale of the tickets was used to restore the violins that survived the Holocaust, which happens at every such concert worldwide. Many classical artists who were camp prisoners were forced, while in the concentration camps, to play classical music for the long lines of naked women and men and children who were standing in line outside the gas chambers, waiting to be gassed to death. That is one reason why some violins did not have owners anymore. The cruel Nazis found ways to dehumanize any human, and many of the artists suffered the same fate as the ones they played for.

Unfortunately most violins did not have owners any more, but surprisingly there were many more violins then I imagined in my wildest dreams. The concert was somber, but there was also a feeling of gratefulness and joy. That morning someone was driving by a synagogue in Nashville on a very busy street and shot at the synagogue. Nobody was hurt, but who are those people who do such things? The shooter was never caught. Every synagogue in Nashville has either been shot at or had somebody plant a bomb that was found before it could do any damage. *Hate*, the most horrible word in any language, seems as if it will never die out. Many synagogues in America have been shot at, even while the Shabbat services were going on, and people died because of the "hate shooters." I am aware and feel terrible that this also happens in churches.

Weekends in Israel that I did not work I most often spent with the Herrmanns. Even though I lived now in Tel Aviv, Hans and I still wrote letters to each other, and we kept seeing each other as well. I could not call him unless in an emergency.

The Herrmanns knew about Hans and me. They were not crazy about my relationship with Hans, but they also did not criticize me or preach moral speeches. As a matter of fact, the Herrmanns and Hans and his wife played bridge together with other mutual friends at least once a month.

I wanted to get into the airline business and got a job at Olympic Airways (OA), the Greek state airline, as a telex operator in Tel Aviv. I was the last person to leave the building where OA had its business offices when we had a flight come in and leave the same evening.

I was responsible for all the airplane info that had to be telexed to Athens (i.e., how many passengers, the fuel required, the special meals or snacks on board, the added weight of the aircraft due to luggage, and the assistance or medical needs of passengers in Athens and passengers making a connection). In other words: statistics.

Once the plane was forty-five minutes from Athens over the Mediterranean, Athens Airport took over communications, and I could lock up and go home. We had only three flights a week. This was from 1966 till 1968, when I changed my life again. When things went wrong, only I could be responsible, and only I was to blame. I did ask for advice and for ideas from the Herrmanns and Hans, but the final decision was mine.

In 1965 the Israeli military caught up with me and ordered me to come to Jerusalem and serve my two years in the military. At that time, I had a furnished room with some elderly couple that was well off and educated. It turned out that the husband (I forgot his name) of the house was a member of the Knesset (Israeli parliament). They often invited me to eat with them. They also spoke German and wanted to help a new immigrant. As long as I could not get an Israeli passport, I was a new immigrant but was considered an Israeli. I went to Jerusalem—about an hour bus ride. There I was told that I had been AWOL for two years and that they could arrest me. I asked them, "Why I was not told about this earlier instead of two years later?" Then they showed me a piece of paper with my signature on it—it said I would serve and had a date on it. So on one of the papers that I was forced to sign on the ship when I first arrived in Haifa as an *olah chadasha* (new immigrant), I committed myself to serve in the Israeli military, only I did not know that I had done so or when I had report to serve. All papers I signed at the time of immigration were in Hebrew; I did not know at that time what I signed. The military started testing me, and I decided not to be able to read Hebrew. For an hour they tried to make me read, and I kept saying that I couldn't read Hebrew. Of course they did not believe me.

They didn't understand that I could speak but could not read. I was let go with a document in my hand that said I promised to come back at a certain date. When I got back to my rented room, the owner's husband was at home. I told them what happened and showed them the paper. I explained that two years in the army would kill my income, since I didn't have family in Israel, because I would have to stop working. This was a serious situation, and I could have wound up in jail. Also, all girls and boys went into the military at age eighteen; I was twenty-five years old and was not willing to change my future because of the military. If I had come to Israel at age eighteen, I would have gladly served. The Knesset member said he would talk to Shimon Perez, who was the head of all Israel's military and minister of war. At one point he also was president. I had to go back to Jerusalem, and I was evaluated by a psychiatrist because they understood that I was lying about my Hebrew. It's pretty difficult to lie if that is something you generally don't do. I am not a liar—I tell only white lies so as not to hurt somebody's feelings. But here, with the military, what I did was telling a big lie when I tried to convince them that I could not read Hebrew. The minister of war, Shimon Perez, wrote a letter of release for me. This letter released me of all military duties. Unfortunately I did not make a copy of this letter. That would be such a unique document to have today! Yes—I received my release papers and never was asked again to serve. Whenever one leaves Israel on an Israeli passport, one has to show a document of permission from the Israeli military that grants permission to leave the country. If an Israeli is an active member of the armed forces, the military will make sure that the person knows where the nearest embassy is in case the person is needed for his or her unit and will have to return to Israel on the next flight.

In 1967 Israel was forced to fight yet another war, which later was called the Six-Day War. It took Israel only four hours to demolish the Egyptian Air Force. Egypt could not get one airplane up because we destroyed its airfield and planes at around 4:00 a.m. By 8:00 a.m. on June 5, 1967, we heard the sirens and left our transportation wherever it stood and looked for cover. We did not know that we were at war yet.

That morning Hans had picked me up and drove me to work. We both ran for cover just three blocks away from my workplace when we heard sirens blaring. The sirens stopped soon, and when I got to the office, my coworkers had already started to put sticky paper on the show windows and office windows to prevent glass from flying in case it broke from bomb attacks.

I had gone through the war in Germany, but I had never been involved in preparation for a full-out war. Here in Israel we were sent home. For me that was where the Herrmanns lived for the full duration of the war.

There was no TV, only the radio. We heard the code names for certain units without knowing who they were or where they were ordered to. Whole units and regiments were ordered to report. But many Israelis already knew where to go. It was very tense. Ilse understood that I was afraid. I sat outside on the stoop and watched the bombs hitting something. At night, in the dark, we realized that Jerusalem was being bombed. And here, we were helpless. All volunteer jobs were filled, so all I could do was watch and pray we all were going to be ok. On the first day of the war, we learned early on that Egypt had been defeated by our air force because it had flown under the radar to Egypt and destroyed all the aircraft Egypt had without touching the plane dummies that were on the airfield. Of course, there still was Sinai, crowded with Egyptian soldiers, but they soon gave up, took off their boots (because they could not run with them), and headed back to Egypt. Egypt was defeated on the third day of the war. The biggest challenge was Jordan. Its soldiers were British trained and fought better than most of the soldiers from other Arab countries.

I lost a friend and colleague on the last day of the war in Old Jerusalem due to a sniper. That was very sad. He had come to Israel from South Africa to work and serve in Israel. We also gained the Golan Heights from Syria. The kibbutz I lived in when I first came to Israel was on the bottom of the Golan Heights, which were mountains high enough to collect some snow in the winter months, and because of that, they were called little Switzerland. Winning those territories did make Israel very proud, and I am indebted to those who lost their lives, because the Syrians caused hell for the kibbutzim below the Golan Heights. My kibbutz was not the only one located in the foothills of the Golan Heights. This was a costly win, as well as the one in Old Jerusalem, for Israel and for the lives lost in order to win. In the late '70s, a friend of mine went to Israel, and when he came back, he proudly told me that he had been on top of the Golan Heights and took a piss toward Syria as a trophy piss, so to speak.

The world soon learned that David had once again slain Goliath!

The tiny country of Israel fought, as always, against five Arab countries all attacking Israel at the same time—but in this war the cherry on top was that we got the Old City of Jerusalem back, which had been lost in 1948 to Jordan when Israel became the State of Israel and was forced to fight its first war with the Arab countries that attacked it. We did not have the weaponry needed to fight that war. But we won the first war in spite of it. We now had the holiest site for the Jews, the Wailing Wall, or as we call it, the Kotel, back in our hands in Old Jerusalem. We defeated five Arab countries—Jordan, Lebanon, Syria, Iraq, and Egypt—in six days. We have had to fight a total of five wars since Israel's establishment in 1948 to date, and we have won each and every one of these wars with a costly number of Israeli lives. But we have never asked any country to help us fight, not even the UN; though we did ask for weapons, we are now capable of making some of our own.

Two days after Old Jerusalem was cleared, nonmilitary people could now go to the Kotel. Hans picked me up and then Ilse Herrmann (Hans's wife didn't want to go), and off we went. It was truly emotional, and I could not even comprehend it, even though I touched the Wall. Tradition is to write a short request or a wish or prayer on a piece of paper and hope it will come true. Those papers are pushed between the crevices of the huge stones of the Wall. The reason why it's considered holy is that it is the outer wall of King Solomon's second temple, after his father King David built the first one and both were destroyed by the Romans. This is the outer wall, which is all that is left of the temple above ground; we know excavations will show more of the temple, and indeed they do. People come to the Wall for different reasons. Number one is that it is the holiest site for the Jewish people, and to have the Wall is a miracle in itself. The Christians come out of respect or curiosity, and the piece of paper pushed between the blocks of stones is pure belief and hope. After all, Solomon's temple is mentioned in the Old Testament. Every time I travel to Israel, a trip to Jerusalem is a must. Last time, in 2017, when I was there, we couldn't go to Old Jerusalem because one crazy, idiotic young Arab terrorist woman stabbed an Israeli female soldier. The terrorist was shot by the Israeli military. Both women survived. But it made my trip to Israel very sad, because Jerusalem was locked down and nobody could go to Old Jerusalem and to the Kotel. That Arab female terrorist had a three-year-old son. She had a note attached to him, which was found by the military, saying for him to make her proud and do what she was doing, going out there and killing Jews. My friends and I followed that report closely. I am glad that the female Israeli soldier was ok after treatment. But I was more than frustrated not to be able to go to Jerusalem's Old City. It is such an exciting place, and once you have been there, it will be clear to you why. Also, I would like to mention that the terrorists that kill or try to kill Israelis and get hurt during an attack are treated by Israeli doctors who save their lives (it's an oxymoron).

Back to Israel and 1967. Since I worked for Olympic Airways, the Greek airline, I was able to get my mother and her husband free tickets from Frankfurt via Athens to Tel Aviv. My mother lived in Munich, so they still had to get themselves to Frankfurt because Olympic Airways did not fly out of Munich. But my mother and husband were still upset about the expense to get from Munich to Frankfurt. I gave up my apartment, which was a studio, for them and I slept at a neighbor's apartment, on the couch. I tried to get as much free time from work as possible, and I made sure they met German-speaking Israelis and arranged sightseeing for them. One thing is worth mentioning: that even though the Herrmanns did not like my mother, just from my telling them about her and how she handled me when I was growing up, they showed up at my apartment to welcome them the day of my mother's arrival because they loved me and they knew how much that meant to me. Two weeks before the Six-Day War that broke out on June 5, 1967, my mother and her husband returned to Germany. My mother wrote me a letter begging me to return to Germany because of the upcoming war and saying that when we were in World War II, at least we were together (which is not true because we were not united until the end of April 1945), and she did not want to lose me. A sentiment I did not appreciate. As they say, "that sentimental letter from my mother came a little too late in my life."

The year 1967 was a year of huge changes for me.

I had a membership to the Hilton swimming pool that year and could use it at any time. One morning, a few days after the Six-Day war, I was there very early, and when I got into the pool, this guy swam up to me and said in a New York accent, "What is an Irish girl doing in Israel?"

I used to have real nice natural red hair, lots of freckles, and green eyes, and my reply came in a harsh tone: "I'm not Irish; I'm an Israeli." He smiled and swam away. Later that day, he asked me whether I wanted to have lunch with him, and I declined, even though I was hungry and could easily have eaten something. This was barely three days after the Six-Day War. Tourists slowly returned to Israel, but most people who were there were journalists. My friend Daliah already had met a British journalist and joined me at the pool, boyfriend in tow. Again I saw this American who had spoken to me earlier, and I got up and said to him, "If your offer still stands, I would like a sandwich." He was pleased, and we went into the hotel coffee shop and ordered some food.

That evening we had dinner and went to the Sheraton Hotel bar for entertainment and drinks. Around 11:00 p.m. I asked him whether he could get a car. Of course I knew he could not rent a car that late in Israel. He said, "I don't have a car," and I suggested using a taxi to drive around in. I knew that it be would be expensive, but he liked the idea, and we hired a taxi that was parked in front of the hotel. I have no clue why I was drawn to this man. I took him to a place outside Tel Aviv, almost to Herzliah, about twenty-five minutes north of Tel Aviv. There was a Greek bar and restaurant that I knew of, but I had never been there before. We went inside and had the taxi driver wait for us. They played Zorba music, as in the film *Zorba*, and

I started to dance the typical Greek dance all alone on the dance floor. Everybody watched, and I did not care. I felt the music and knew the steps; after all, my name is Greek, and my father was Greek, and I have been to Greece several times. Somehow the Greek blood flows in my veins. Therefore I did not make a fool of myself; the opposite happened. People applauded and whistled once I stopped when the music stopped. I think Bernie Shapiro—that was his name—was impressed. We went on to other bars, and at 4:00 a.m. I finally arrived at my apartment building. He got his jacket, as if he would come up, but I said, "Please don't," and he respected that.

He then said, "Can I pick you up on Saturday evening?" I said yes and told him that I was working and would not get off until 9:00 p.m. He said that was fine and asked me the address of my job, and I said, "Olympic Airways." I figured that if he wanted it badly enough he would find a way to find that address. This was Friday morning, and I was very perplexed that he did not make a date for Friday night. But then I realized that he most likely had a date, made before he met me, with another girl that he did not want to break.

At 9:00 p.m. on Saturday evening, the taxi was in front of Olympic Airways just as I was closing. Bernie was waiting in the open door of the taxi. We had dinner and went back to the Hilton, where he stayed. When we got to his room, he started to feel ill and asked me whether I could get a medical doctor. I called the front desk that used a doctor on call. The doctor admitted him to a hospital via ambulance. I did not go with him. I called him the next day, and he said he was feeling better. I visited him in the hospital that same afternoon with an English newspaper, the *Jerusalem Post*, in my hands. I think he was glad to see me because he had no friends or family in Israel take care of him.

He was released that same afternoon, and from that day on, till the day of his departure, we spent every minute possible together. Only on the last day of his stay in Israel did I spend the night with him at his hotel. In the morning, when his flight from Lod Airport took off, I accompanied him to the airport by taxi and he gave me some money to take a taxi back to town. As a farewell present, I bought him a record of the latest hit in Israel, which was "Jerusalem of Gold" ("Jerushalayim schel sahav").

I did tell Hans about Bernie and that I would visit him in New York City. Bernie did not know that I had planned a trip to visit him in New York City, but I had a free ticket coming from Olympic Airways and vacation time. The first letter I received from Bernie was pretty cold and also not inviting. I was very disappointed because I was not the kind of girl that slept around. I thought that the night we had spent together meant something to him, also because we had spent a lot of time together. But it obviously was not that meaningful to him. But I had my plan to go and see him in New York City and had never told him in my letters about my plan. I requested my free ticket and vacation time and went to the American embassy to get my visa. The form I had to fill out asked why I wanted to go to New York City, and I wrote, "to visit my fiancé." I did that in my stupidity, which caused all kinds of problems. The consul asked to talk to me and asked me all kinds of personal questions. I did not know that a fiancé visa was a whole different thing and needed all kinds of paperwork from the actual fiancé; it's called a K-1 visa. Well, I finally had to be honest and say I was seeing my boyfriend. I also had to prove that I had a return ticket and a job to come back to and that I had no intentions of staying in New York City, and then I finally got my tourist visa. I hadn't heard from Bernie for weeks, and it was now September, and the last time we had seen each other was in June. I had the guts to call him collect and tell him that I would arrive in New York City on a specific date and flight, not really giving him a choice. He seemed ok with that, and I got very excited to take this trip. I had always been curious about New

York City but even more about Bernie and whether or not we could have a relationship.

Since I was honest with Hans, I did not have any sexual relationship with him from that time on, even when he visited me in my apartment. It felt strange, but I knew this was the only honest way to deal with it, because I thought that maybe I could fall in love with Bernie, the man in New York City.

I always was a one-man's woman and was honest about it. Loving Hans was the most important thing to me. It was an emotional, positive love as much as physical. But the tenderness he taught me and the emotional caring for eight years were the most important and most impactful happenings in my life. I still carry that with me, even today. I am so deeply grateful to Hans for his support in cultivating me and his making me understand things about humanity and the generosity of giving—not materialistic giving but emotional giving, something I never knew about before I met Hans. I loved Hans from the moment I saw him, when I first met him in the hallway of the building where my friends lived, and he was with his wife, in Berlin in 1958.

I never forgot him, even for the full year when he was back in Israel. I didn't even know where he came from, but I loved the soft tenderness in his face and wanted so badly to be kissed by him. I remember Hans being in shock when he realized that he loved me. It was something he had not planned on, but it happened, and it was wonderful to be so deeply loved and receive those beautiful love letters; I still have some of them today. We were like teenagers madly in love, and the experience was something I would not want to give up as part of my life. I loved this man for eight years, and out of that, he loved me for at least five years. Of course he was fighting his own feelings, but then he had to give in, and we made the most of it. We wrote many letters to each other, even when I lived in Tel Aviv on the same street he lived on. I did not have a phone and could not always call him—after all, his wife could pick up the phone. She knew about us, but I did not complicate that delicate situation.

But Hans said himself that I should find a man who could possibly marry me. When I met Bernie, I never thought I would love him. I liked the idea of him being able to afford things, but I did not know that he was a millionaire. Well, he was. When I arrived in New York City in September 1967, merely three months after the Six-Day War in Israel, he picked me up in his Lincoln Continental, and I kept asking him, "What kind of car is this?" I did not think that a car was named after President Lincoln, but here it was. I also did not understand why such an expensive-looking car did not have a door handle or offer the ability to manually roll down the window! I did not want to seem stupid and ignorant, so I just watched how he opened the doors and if needed rolled down the window. (I was that new to modern life in New York City.) When we arrived in Manhattan, at his condo building, on the East Side, next to Gracie's Mansion (I had no clue that the mayor of New York lived there), I was overwhelmed, trying not to show it of course. There were a doorman and an elevator man, and I didn't have to do anything. The view from his condo overlooked the East River and Brooklyn Bridge, which was a beautiful view. I never got tired of it. It was strange that Hans had taught me all the values of a human being and this guy Bernie showed me the other side of Cinderella's life. The one where one can afford anything and everything.

I was totally unaware of his wealth and the way he lived and the things he was able to afford to spoil me with. When I saw his king-size bed, I was amazed—what a beautiful bedroom he had, and the comfort of the bed was amazing, totally new to me. In Tel Aviv I slept on a pull-out couch. His living room was spacious, with a dining area and a balcony that faced the East River, and of course there was a kitchen. Not knowing about Dorothy's rainbow and the yellow brick road, I still was definitely not in Israel anymore.

I had landed in the very land of all possibilities without knowing it.

Everything amazed me. The stores, the theaters, the restaurants, and the avenues were so amazing to me. Fifth Avenue and Lexington Avenue became my favorite places to go to window shop. Everything looked expensive, but I couldn't grab the richness and value of those shops. But I learned fast. Who cannot be in awe of Rockefeller Center? Even today it amazes me. On top of the RCA Building was a restaurant called the Rainbow Room, which was Duke Ellington's playground and where he performed. How exciting that was!

The day that I arrived, we had dinner in the Lexington Hotel restaurant and bar, which had live entertainment. The entertainment was a Spanish dancer by the name of El Greco, whom I knew from movies where he danced his classic Spanish bolero tap dance. It was wonderful and beautiful, and I felt so special. I had never thought I would meet famous people that close up.

The first couple of days I was on my own; Bernie drove to New Jersey, where his company was. He came home after work, and we went to eat at real nice restaurants, and when we came home we made love and started to get to know each other. It became very clear to me very soon that this man would be important in my life and that I was starting to more than like him. I knew that I was falling in love but did not dare to say so. I did not want to frighten Bernie. I didn't know him that well yet. On the third day or so, he told me that his sister Dotty would come by and take me shopping. Well, she came and was very nice and friendly, and I really liked her, and then she took me shopping. I did not know about Bloomingdale's or Lord & Taylor and Saks and all the shops on Fifth Avenue, but she did, and that is where she took me shopping. It was amazing. When I found a dress that I liked, she would call Bernie and come back and say, "Let's buy that for you if you like it," and like it I did. My first dress was what they call a little black dress. I did not know what that meant, but I soon understood.

In the mornings before Bernie went to work, he would leave some money on the dresser and say, "If you find something you like, buy it." I spent a lot of time in Bloomingdale's. I would ask the doorman of the building Bernie lived in to get a taxi for me and then would take off shopping. On my own I was able to shop for beautiful undergarments and nightgowns. Bernie was pleased that I had good taste and trusted me shopping by myself. After all I had a good teacher that showed me where to go, namely Dotty. On weekends we would eat out elegantly and then see a Broadway show. After that, we would go home and make love, not sex but love. Caring, soft, tender love, something that was kind of new to Bernie. But it felt great, and I looked forward to those nights or mornings. He did not like to shop or go to stores, so I went grocery shopping across the street from where he lived and had the groceries delivered. I went shopping with his sister a lot. One day I was coat shopping, and I had seen a beautiful green suede coat but I also needed an elegant black coat for evenings, something classy and dressy. I found one that was very classy and right for the theater and dressy for dinners. I could not decide which one to choose, and I told Dotty, who was with me, that I liked both and couldn't make a decision. She called Bernie. They talked for a moment, and when she came back, she said, "Why don't we buy both!" Wow. This was at Lord & Taylor. The green coat was made in Israel, and the black had a label that was not known to me at that time. So we purchased both coats. We are talking several hundred dollars for both coats. I never did know how much each of them was. I just knew I was in heaven and in love. Everything I purchased Dotty put on a credit card, and I am sure Bernie somehow made good on those charges. I did not have a credit card—just a few dollars in cash for small purchases. When Bernie came home that night, I modeled both coats for him, and he liked both.

One night he did not feel well and asked me to find a doctor in the building. I called the doorman, and he told me that one resident was an ophthalmologist and gave me the apartment number. When I spoke to the doctor, he said that he was a specialist for eyes, and I said that I knew that but my friend felt as if he was having a heart attack. I finally convinced him to go with me and have a look at Bernie and figure out what was wrong. Bernie already had called his brother Don in New Jersey to come and pick him up, which he did. The doctor said it was not the heart and maybe he had had a panic attack. As the doctor was leaving, Bernie kissed me goodbye and said to me, "I love you." Then his brother arrived and took him to his home in Jersey. I was left alone with this overwhelming feeling of being loved by the man I already was in love with, though I had never told him. It was an amazing feeling, and I had nobody to share my excitement with. I barely slept that night and kept hugging Bernie's pillow. Here I was, Little Miss Nobody, and I had two men that loved me. How much luckier could I get?

I thought of Hans and his love, but this was different, and one was nothing to compare with the other. Two different men and two different loves—both absolutely beautiful, each in its own way. I didn't want to have missed either one of those loves in my life. It also was not a competition, because both loves were so special.

The next morning, I couldn't wait to call Bernie's brother Don's house to find out how Bernie was doing and talk to him. Bernie was doing fine. He was still asleep at 9:00 a.m. He always needed a lot of sleep, and I was always up very early. I walked around in his apartment making coffee and waited for Bernie to wake up. Finally, close to noontime, Bernie called me, and all I could say was, "Do you know what you said to me last night before you left?"

And he said very calmly, "Of course I do. I told you that I love you." He said that in such a way that it was understood without saying that he loved me. I told him I was still on cloud nine, because I loved him so much myself but hadn't had the guts to say it, because I thought it would scare him away.

One day before my flight back to Israel, he told me that he had invited his family to his place and ordered some catering because he wanted them to meet me. That was on a Saturday afternoon, and I said to him, "I want one thing from you."

He said, "Let me write on a piece of paper what it is that you want." So he wrote on the paper "RING," and

I said, "how did you know?" Because that was exactly what I wanted. On Shabbat afternoon, he drove to the diamond district, which was mostly Jewish-owned stores. He asked for the ring I was wearing (which was given to me by Hans for my hotel graduation). When Bernie came back with a ring, I was in awe, because it was exactly what I wanted. It was an eternity diamond ring with diamonds all around the ring, just like a wedding band. He told me that he did not want me to wear the ring when his family showed up, a request I honored. Bernie never before had introduced a girl to his family (except his ex-wife). This was almost like introducing his future wife—at least that's what I thought it meant. I met the parents and all the brothers. Don, the oldest, I already had met before, and his wife. But Stanley, the baby brother, and his wife I met for the first time, and then there was Dotty and her husband. Since my flight left at 10:00 p.m. I asked Bernie not to have his family over for long, since I wanted some alone time with him before leaving his apartment. The moment they left, I put the ring that Bernie bought me that day back on. Since I had already packed the suitcases, I had to add one, because the one I had brought with me was not enough for the return trip to Israel, since I had bought quite a few things and I wanted to take all my new clothing with me.

We had plenty of time for our last lovemaking. But then it was time to leave the apartment and drive to JFK Airport to catch my flight. It was amazing how fast the three weeks' vacation passed. I was, of course, sad to leave, but I also was happy that I had had a wonderful time, and I was filled with love and hope that Bernie would call me and tell me to come back to New York City and that we would be together forever. Before we left, we had a serious conversation about our age difference. Bernie was fourteen years older than I was. He was concerned that he might not be able to keep up with me as we got older. For me, there was no problem. He knew everything about me, including about Hans and me. I told him that we did not have to get married; I would be happy just to live with him, as long as we were together. Marriage was something very far from his mind and not a good subject. He was divorced and just was in no mood to try marriage again. To him, living together was the same as marriage; the obligation of a full-time partnership scared him. He wanted to feel free and come and go whenever he pleased. All that was not understood by me; I did understand at a later time, but only years later. He gave me an envelope that said "Open when airborne." The moment I found my seat and sat down, I opened that envelope. He did say in that card he had written that he loved me. My heart was full with love for him, and I was hoping that I would soon see him again. But I also was excited to be back in Israel, and I was looking forward to going to work the next day and showing off my new wardrobe and the ring he gave me.

In the late '60s it was a luxury to have a telephone. You could request one, which meant your name was put on a waiting list and it could take years before you finally got the phone. Bernie either had to call me at work or I would call him collect when I was at the Herrmanns.

In between calls, we wrote loving letters to each other. I was trying to understand what was truly happening. I did believe that we were meant for each other, and I was not willing to just lie down and play dead. I was not ready to give up. This was a very hard time for me, and I was lucky I had the Herrmanns to help me to handle this situation. I was crushed and needed to find a way to make it work. Hans and I at that time stopped seeing each other.

In early spring of 1968, I signed up to become a stewardess for El Al, which had started a new course for young, good-looking, educated people to start training at the stewardess training school. One had to speak at least three languages, which I did: English, German, and Hebrew. Qualifying also meant knowing how to carry yourself and how you dressed for the initial interview. The qualification also included that you had to be no less then 5'4" and weigh no more than 126 pounds.

I went to the top manager of Olympic Airways and requested to be put on the late shift, only so I could attend the El Al training classes during the day. Like most of the airline managers, he had emigrated from Germany and spoke German very well. Mr. Kern said to me, "If it weren't for your beautiful eyes, I would have fired you a long time ago, so I will let you work the evening shift so you can become a stewardess." I always was complimented about my green eyes, which went great with my red hair, and men and women mentioned them often. At one time, at a contest, I was voted the woman with the most beautiful eyes. I had also had a photo shoot for the cover of an Israeli magazine.

The training at the stewardess school included learning how to walk and talk, how to use makeup properly, and how to have good manners—in short, etiquette. Because if one wore the uniform of the airline, one did not represent just the airline but also the country it represented. They did not want us to make a bad impression in any way, anywhere. Even in our private lives, after all, we represented the State of Israel. But the most important training was in emergency procedures by land and by sea. Every commercial aircraft has certain areas where the rescue equipment is kept, and we needed to know what each of them did. If a student failed the emergency procedure on the final test, that student was let go. First aid and emergencies were the principal test that one could not fail at.

I aced the stewardess school final test, and my first assignment was on a training flight to no other destination than New York City, with a two-day layover in Paris. I felt fortunate and anxious because now I had to let Bernie know that I would be in New York. The flight stopped in Paris, France, and we had a two-day layover. The experienced crew took us "greenhorns" under their wings, and they were really nice with us new crew members. Our hotel in Paris was right around The Arc de Triump and Champs-Élysées, the main avenue in Paris. This was a perfect area to be in, "in the heart of Paris." At nighttime the avenue is illuminated with all-white lights, which made it look so special and romantic and elegant. It looked just like a postcard, only this was the real thing. We had an allowance for meals, and the hotel was paid directly by El Al. The other great thing was that I got a telephone within days of completing my training, courtesy of the airline, so that the schedulers could get ahold of me in case there were itinerary changes, which happened quite often. The monthly fee for the phone was paid by El Al, but the usage of the phone was my responsibility. I decided not to call Bernie but to wait until I got to JFK and call him from there. After two days in Paris, it was on to another plane with the crew we flew in to Paris, which happened every time we had a layover. The crew that flew in from Tel Aviv to a European city was changed with my crew, which already was in the European city, and we, in return, continued the nonstop flight to JFK. On transatlantic flights we had to serve two meals because it took more than six hours to reach New York. We also served drinks and beverages of all kinds. At that time we did not have in-flight movies. After we served lunch, we, the trainees, were quizzed by a trainer that we knew from the classroom about our knowledge of time changes and what countries or cities we were flying over and about the currency and other general questions from the material that was part of our training. I felt very confident and had no problem answering all the questions. Maybe I was even a little too eager!

As soon as we landed in JFK and went through customs and immigration, I looked for a phone to call Bernie. I called him collect, since I did not have American coins to use in the phone. I reached him in his office and told him that I was in JFK, on my way to Midtown Manhattan. He told me to take a taxi and come to his condo. The airlines provided us with limos for pickup from the airport to the hotel and vice versa. I was super excited but also nervous. I dropped my stuff off at the hotel, changed clothes, and hurried to get a taxi to get to East River Drive. When I arrived at Bernie's building, I rode up to the tenth floor and rang the doorbell. He opened the door in his dress pants and T-shirt (he did not own any jeans) and told me to come in. Since it was late September, I wore the black coat he had bought me during my last visit. We chitchatted for a while, and then he suggested that we get something to eat. To my surprise we walked two blocks (we always took a car even for short distances), and we went to my favorite Italian restaurant. He put some money into the hand of the headwaiter, and we were seated immediately. I ordered my favorite dish, veal parmesan. We just sat there not talking about anything important, almost as if we were never apart. But it was almost a year since I had last seen him. He never asked why I was in New York, and I was not volunteering any info. I had my plan for when to tell him. As we were walking home, he suddenly pulled me into his arms, and we kissed, and it was the same sensation that we both felt, just as if we said hello only yesterday. When we got to the apartment, we could not wait to make love. Again, it felt just like yesterday. I finally asked him—didn't he want to know why I was in New York? When I told him that I was a stewardess for El Al, he was impressed. He had always dated women that had careers and impressed people by the way they dressed and kept themselves up. It took me a long time to understand and finally see that. He had dated models and Wall Street brokers, and they all were very pretty and drew attention to themselves; that's what impressed him. If I had understood that earlier, I would have saved myself a lot of unnecessary pain. Whenever I got to New York, I spent my time at Bernie's. That went on for a good year, and we seemed happy—at least I thought so.

I went to an ob-gyn in Israel, who told me that I was pregnant. I went to the Herrmanns' house and told them, and I said I would call Bernie and tell him. Bernie's first question was "Is it mine?" It was! He asked me to get an abortion and move to New York, and he said we could have a child after we got married. I told him that I wanted this child and that I had to talk to the Herrmanns before I said yes to an abortion. The Herrmanns were not crazy about the abortion part, but they explained that it was my life and my decision. I asked Ilse if after the procedure I could recuperate at her house, and she said, "Only if you don't tell the girls what kind of procedure you had and why you are recovering here." I contemplated my situation and decided to have the abortion, but I was not proud of myself. I knew that I had to give up my stewardess job. This was a bittersweet decision, but I loved Bernie so much, and I believed him. I gave up my apartment and had some of my stuff shipped to New York, since I would be living in New York. Three months after I moved in with Bernie, he told me I had to leave, that he had made a mistake. Within a week's time of his telling me that I had to leave, I was on a plane to Tel Aviv without any money or any future that I could think of. I was penniless and homeless, since I had sublet my apartment, and of course I was terribly hurt. I also felt shame that I had let a man do this to me and about how blind I was. I arrived in Tel Aviv and went to a very low-class hotel that Bernie booked for me (the millionaire that lived only in high-class style booked an extremely cheap hotel for me) for only enough days for me to find a place to move into. I eventually got a furnished room with the same people that I had rented my studio from, which was signed for a year by the new tenant. I was too ashamed to show my face at my friends' place or to even contact them with just a phone call. More than anything I needed a job. The airline was the only business I knew, but Israel is small, and word gets around if and where a job is available.

I had been in this situation before, and I knew that I had to get myself together and face the music and just be honest and move on. I never really forgave Bernie for how he handled this situation—and how cold does a person have to be to do what he did? It took me eight months to get my life back to normal, or rather what I call normal. I still had my friends and a job with an airline. It was time, again, to start a new beginning. I had done it before—I had lost everything—but I was strong enough to do it again and came out with my head held high.

# Epilogue

I had American friends in Tel Aviv who owned a bar, and I went there often as a customer and also to help out when needed. I was friends with many regulars at the bar. One day this stranger walked in and asked if he could have a margarita cocktail. My friends were out of town, and the regular barmaid did not know how to fix this drink. So I volunteered to make the drink on the condition that he would buy me one as well. Which he did! That is how I met Jessie Jackson Bateman from Tennessee—at that time I had no idea where that was. He was in Tel Aviv to assist the Israeli Air Force as a consultant, sent there by the company in America he worked for. We started dating, and after about six months, I found an apartment and we moved in together. I kept my job, but he paid for the household expenses. Within a year's time, his contract ended, and he had to go back to the States with a stop in Hamburg. I was in Israel for my best friend's wedding, which she had on my birthday, and about a month later, Jessie and I and the car he had bought in Israel took a ship from Haifa to Piraeus, Greece, with stops at all the Mediterranean islands along the cruise. When we stopped at Cyprus, we got married. After a few days in Greece we drove to Petra, which is a Greek port city that mostly ferries between Greek islands and Italy. It took 24 hours on the ferry to get to Brindisi, Italy. We had our car on board.

We drove up the Italian west coast with many stops at interesting sites. This trip from Haifa to Germany took us 30 days. We also included other countries besides Italy like Monaco, the Cote Azures, Switzerland, and Austria in to Munich, Germany, where my mother lived.

We found out that our marriage license was not accepted in Germany or America. We wanted to elope in Germany... only because my mother lived there.

We went to the Standes Amt (marriage license bureau) with my mother in tow. There they asked for my birth certificate which was issued to my TANA name, just like the Nazis ordered it. My passport was issued to Kassiana. But the clerk said "if you can not show me a birth certificate with Kassiana on it, there is no chance that you will get married in Germany." We showed him the letter we received from the office of statistics that declared my name officially anywhere is Kassiana. The letter was issued in 1947 but that did not help, this clerk was not changing his mind (damn Nazi). Jessie decided to apply for a fiancée, or K1, visa.

This visa allows one to get married within 90 days, once one entered the USA. The American embassy had no problem with my paperwork, which I had professionally translated into English and certified.

I received my visa within a month's time. I didn't know at that time that I was pregnant with my son.

We departed to the USA and settled in Nashville where a few month later I delivered a boy we call Lee.

I love my son very much and promised to never slap him and to let him know how much his parents love him. We always had an open and tender relationship with lots of affection and letting him know every day how much he is loved. Even today when we speak on the phone our last sentence is I LOVE YOU. Every night way into my son's early teens I would sit on the edge of his bed, singing to him the same lullaby, tucked him in and kissed him and wished him a good night and so did his dad.

I made sure not to follow into my mother's footsteps and repeat her mistakes, and I succeeded. My son is able to give his daughter the same loving care and attention with love and patience.

My husband wanted me to stay home and not work the first 5 years of our son's life, he said it's more important then getting  job. I stayed home until my son started school.

I eventually started working at a travel agent as an international consultant. Flying around the world came in handy at that time.

I also wanted to do some volunteer work and after speaking to different social workers I decided on the Crisis Intervention Center where I volunteered for 12 years. I involved myself in social programs and also was a speaker for the United Way as a child suicidal prevention councilor and other volunteer work. I received numerous awards, including a plaque from the German consulate for helping a German student get back home after being involved in a bad car accident. He did not know English well and I was able to translate and find resources to get him home. I was interviewed by television and newspapers where columns were written about my volunteer work. All together I volunteered 20 years in different social agencies.

I am proud not to have become anything like my mother and I was able to teach my son true motherly love and for him to pass on this parental love to his daughter, Maya, who is now a sophomore in high school. I am very proud of my little family.

I can truly say that I am proud to not be my mother's daughter.

Printed in the USA
CPSIA information can be obtained
at www.ICGtesting.com
LVHW010602190823
755497LV00013B/647

9 798885 903660